UNTOLD STORIES
VOL. 1

CGST and Its Transformational Impact

C. RUTH TAYLOR
Foreword by Stan Gerig

Extra MILE Innovators
Kingston, Jamaica W.I.

.   .   .   .   .   .

Published by:
Extra MILE Innovators
21 Phoenix Avenue,
Kingston 10, Jamaica W.I.
www.extramileja.com

Editor: Grace Gordon
Cover Designer: Pro-marketer, Adedolapo

Author Contact
For consultation, feedback or speaking engagements,
contact the author at ruthtaylor@extramileja.com or
contact CGST at https://cgst.edu.jm/.

To the Gerig family,
all Caribbean agents of transformation
and all CGST's Ambassadors,
May your legacy inspire generations yet unborn for the glory of God.

Book Review

Dr. David Corbin, former President of the Caribbean Graduate School of Theology (2017-2020)

The author of this volume is a brilliant archivist. She has superbly identified, appraised, preserved, arranged, described and provided access to significant historical material. This volume competently attempts to empower upcoming generations to continue spreading the flame of transformation.

Her agents of transformation, all graduates of the Caribbean Graduate School of Theology, were accurately described as legacy builders. Having studied with many of these agents of change, we students never imagined the impact any of us would have had on others in the upcoming decades.

One of the things many of us students had in common was the influence of visionary Dr. Zenas Gerig. It was Dr. Gerig's phone call to me in 1971 that changed my career path. As you read the stories of my colleagues and legacy builders, many will concur that their contact with Dr. Gerig also influenced their lives and career paths. Hence, the inclusion of Dr. Gerig's pioneering story is most appropriate.

This volume reminds me of God's words to Moses in Exodus. The Amalekites had just been defeated in battle. Moses' obedience to God's battle-plan was mainly responsible for that victory. To ensure that Joshua and upcoming generations were aware of His plan, God instructed Moses *to write this on a scroll as something to be remembered...* (Exodus 17:14, NIV).

Author Ruth Taylor followed that injunction in crafting this volume. The legacy of her "agents of transformation," will continue for many years, among those who dare to read these pages. Like me, I believe you will be informed and transformed.

Foreword

"Big Up Jesus!"

It is an honour as Dr. Zenas Gerig's youngest son to write a foreword to the first volume of *Untold Stories, the CGST edition*. Within CGST's rich history, there certainly are many rich stories to be told!

One such story, not widely known, pertains to my father who was asked to write an entry for a daily devotional titled "This Cloud of Witnesses," published in 1999 by Taylor University. If ever there was an opportunity to share his heart with as many people as possible, this was his opportunity.

He titled his devotional, "Big Up Jesus." In it he shared his life verse, Philippians 3:10 that says, "I want to know Christ and the power of his resurrection and the fellowship of sharing in his sufferings, becoming like him in his death."

He then emphasized that if the Apostle Paul, in spite of his dramatic conversion, his great achievements and his fruitful ministry needed to know Christ more, certainly we do too—even more so!

He concluded the devotional with a couple of illustrations gleaned from his years in Jamaica, namely that it is not uncommon when getting on a Jamaican bus to hear, **"Small up yourselves!"**, and when gathering together for worship in church to hear, **"Let's big up Jesus!"** He pointed out that these two expressions are in line with the driving passions of Paul's heart and those of John the Baptist who declared, "He must increase, but I must decrease."

Those who knew my father knew he was not flashy, but faithful; faithful to accomplish the tasks he was asked to do for Jesus and His Kingdom's sake. Both he and my mother came from humble farm families that didn't live just to farm, but to serve Jesus.

Once married, they sought to 'big up Jesus' in the same way. My father's conversion to Christ, his early home-church ministry, his attending Bible College and seminary, his decisions to become a missionary, to go to Jamaica, to pastor, to attend Indiana University for a better education, to start two institutions of evangelical higher learning, to serve on numerous boards, to write multiple bylaws for multiple organizations, to help start evangelical organizations, were all done at the requests and guidance of others.

He only went on to get a doctorate at Indiana University because his guidance counsellor said he could do so by just adding a few courses to his master's degree and that it would be helpful for what he was called to do in higher education.

Speaking of 'not flashy', I can remember sitting in multiple church pews as my parents travelled to raise support, listening to my father speak, thinking, "He's not that eloquent." Rev. David Clark, the field director of the Jamaican Missionary Church at the time my parents first came to the island, said when he met my father his thought was, "This isn't the man for the job!"

Gloria Noelliste, wife of Dr. Dieumeme Noelliste who led both schools for 20 years, said in a tribute to my father, "If you were anywhere in a crowd of leaders and asked, 'Will the real PhD. please stand up?' Dr. Gerig would be slow to stand."

Added to this, I heard that at times when leaders of worldwide organizations acquainted with my father's work first met him, their thought was, "Him?" The answer? "Yes, him. Because of Him! Jesus!" As with Paul and John the Baptist, remarkable things can be done when we "small up ourselves" and "big up Jesus."

Is this not true of our best life stories, if the truth be told? So also, as CGST's untold stories are now told in this volume, we will be hearing the stories of Jesus working through the lives of many of his servants. What a great opportunity to **Big up Jesus!**

For His sake,

Stan Gerig,
Acting Chairman, CGST Board,
Son of Dr. Zenas Gerig

Table of Contents

Introduction

"Remember your leaders, who spoke the word of God to you. Consider the outcome of their way of life and imitate their faith."—Hebrews 13:7, NIV

What is life if not measured by its impact? Dr. Zenas Gerig was a prime mover in theological education in the Caribbean. His impact as a transformational leader positioned Caribbean society for lasting change. He made this impact by investing in Christian higher education and the development of Christian leaders for service to the church and the wider society. After five decades, the government of Jamaica recognized his contribution and awarded him one of the nation's highest awards on National Heroes Day in 2001.

In this volume of *Untold Stories,* we delve further into the story of Dr. Zenas Gerig to learn more about the flame that burned so brightly in his heart. From whence did it come? What was the spark that created this flame? What

1

was it that drove him to work like he did and to make such a lasting impact?

In our research, we discovered a powerful and inspirational story which not only answers these questions, but gives us fuel to preserve his legacy and spread the flame of transformation. His untold story is truly a God-story worthy of publishing among the nations. We further follow the trail of his impact through one of the entities he founded, the Caribbean Graduate School of Theology (CGST) which has become a guardian of the flame that burnt brightly in Dr. Gerig's heart.

As a graduate of CGST, along with other graduates, I am now a carrier of his flame of transformation, and we want to pass it on. As we seek to pass on this flame of transformation, we want you to reflect on these two questions:

How much difference can one person make?

How much of a difference can you make within and beyond the borders of your country or region?

Untold Stories Vol. 1 brings to light the story, impact and legacy of one man whose work has multiplied even in his death, transcending generations, continents, nationalities, races and multiple spheres of influence. It showcases the profiles of 12 of CGST's outstanding graduates (flame carriers) from its first 20 graduations (1989–2009), and testimonials of impact from the latest graduating class (2020). The graduate profiles are inspirational. They include personal testimonies; academic achievements before and after CGST; and service to church, community and country.

Each graduate answers nine questions, including the all-important one about Dr. Gerig's impact on their lives. Many of CGST's graduates have served in non-religious sectors such as counselling, business and finance, law, the security forces and education; some serving beyond the shores of their native country and region.

As a graduate of CGST, I also share my story of impact. This book reaffirms the mission and ethos of CGST, a guardian of Dr. Gerig's flame. I hope Dr. Gerig's story and the stories and achievements of CGST's flame carriers will light the fire of transformation in your heart, and cause you to support CGST in preserving Dr. Gerig's mission of seeing the transformation of Caribbean societies for the glory of God.

1.

What is Untold Stories?

"A people without the knowledge of their past history,
origin and culture is like a tree without roots."
—Marcus Garvey

D r. Las Newman, in taking the reins as the second indigenous president of CGST, made the following remarks in an interview with Mark Dawes, which was published in the Jamaica Gleaner.

I am concerned about a few things in the expansion of the menu. First, the loss of Christian heritage. The Church has been in the Caribbean for 500 years and has left behind some significant pieces of heritage that have been at the base of the fabric of our country. How can we recover that? It is the role of a theological institution to identify those pieces of our heritage that are distinctly religious…I want to see more research on the impact of the church in the community, and how the church can be a significant part of national development going forward.

The *Untold Stories* book series is a legacy building, inspirational catalyst for change. It chronicles the impact of significant people and places in the Caribbean (agents of transformation) whose stories are powerful but not well known. The intent is to empower generations to come, to continue their work and spread the flame of transformation. For the Christian community, it answers in part Dr. Newman's desire to prevent the loss of Christian heritage, thus playing an archival role.

This series is also part of my Abundant Collective, an effort to chronicle and expose the good in "Nazareth" (unlikely places). Future volumes will capture stories of persons from Inner Cities and humble beginnings to show that transformation is possible. This series will provide role models from ordinary walks of life, whose stories perhaps would not otherwise be told because they are not famous or wealthy historical persons.

Through *Untold Stories,* we are intentionally seeking to change the narrative of derogatory cultural perceptions of Third World/Developing countries and the Africa Diaspora. The people of the Caribbean and the African Diaspora are people of significance, and it is up to us to tell our stories and change the narrative.

Dr. Zenas Gerig believed in the greatness of our Caribbean people. Although he was a foreigner, he saw the beauty, abundance and potential of our people. He therefore empowered our people to lead especially through higher Christian education.

Untold Stories Vol. 1 pays tribute to Dr. Gerig and one of the schools he founded, the Caribbean Graduate School of Theology (CGST). It also pays tribute to CGST's outstanding graduates and legacy builders.

The Significance of Volume One

This volume seeks to identify a piece of our heritage that is not only distinctly religious, but shows the impact of Christian education in different spheres of Caribbean society beyond the spiritual. In times of crisis the critics often ask, "What is the church doing?" This book shows the church at work through a Christian institution and the work of its graduates. *Untold Stories Vol. 1* not only points to moments of impact of the church in the distant past, but highlights its contemporary influence and the service of Christian leaders within the church and the wider society.

This kind of storytelling is part of an ongoing commitment to the Congress of Evangelicals in the Caribbean (CONECAR'S) mission to move the Caribbean from mission field to mission force. I believe writing is one way to do that and as we publish God's glory among the nations and tell of his mighty acts (1 Chronicles 16:24; Psalm 96:3; Isaiah 12: 4-5), people will be saved and lives transformed.

God willing, there will be more tales of transformation and these books will support individuals and entities making a difference in the Caribbean. The *Untold Stories* series will preserve their legacies, and change future generations for the glory of God.

7

Part I:
It Only Takes a Spark

Dr. Zenas and Esther Gerig

Note: Although Dr. Gerig is the inspiration for this edition, and the one who got the national award, it was a couple's effort. Without Mrs. Gerig's contribution, he could not have achieved all that he did.

2.

Zenas Gerig's Flame

There are three things that are never satisfied,
four that never say, 'Enough!'...
the grave, the barren womb, land, which is never satisfied with
water, and fire, which never says, 'Enough!'
—Proverbs 30:15b-16, NIV

What is the fire that never says enough? Whatever it is, this is the kind we are lighting by sharing the incredible story of Dr. Zenas Gerig and those of CGST's outstanding graduates. Although I never met Dr. Gerig, I was at his memorial service in 2011 at Grace Missionary Church, and his life and legacy impressed me. Little did I know then, that God had ignited a fire in my heart with his story, and I would one day be writing a book dedicated to him.

Dr. Gerig has shaped much of my personal, academic, spiritual and professional development through the

11

institutions he founded, both of which I had the privilege of attending. He possessed a fire that never said "Enough," as he carried out his life's work. Perhaps the spark of this fire was his miraculous beginnings, first brought to my attention by Vol. 1 of the Caribbean Journal of Evangelical Theology (CJET) in 1997. Those miraculous beginnings once again appeared in a tribute written in 2002 by Dr. Delano Palmer, one of the first graduates of CGST.

Many students, graduates and even lecturers of the schools he founded are unfamiliar with this powerful story about Dr. Zenas Gerig. But it gives us insight into the flame that blazed in his heart from an early age. This *untold story* reveals that he was no ordinary child, and seemed destined to be used by God greatly. As you read his story, may you not only be inspired, but may you also catch the fire that was in Dr. Zenas Gerig's heart and pass it on.

A Miraculous Resurrection and Preservation

The story told by Stan Gerig (Dr. Gerig's youngest son) and others, is that Zenas was pronounced dead at birth by the attending physician. One of his aunts, who was present, did not accept the doctor's diagnosis. She therefore wrapped baby Zenas in a blanket and took him by the wood stove to warm him up. Shortly after, she saw him take his first breath.

Whenever I hear this story, I often think of how Moses' parents saw that he was a fine child and did all they could to preserve his life. Perhaps his aunt had received a divine insight into the future of baby Zenas and this influenced her actions, which brought him back to life. But that was just one of two instances of Dr. Gerig shafting death at an early age.

In Dr. Palmer's tribute to Dr. Gerig in CJET, 2002 edition, we learn,

> Two years later, Zenas barely survived another brush with death when he was run over by the large metal wheel of a hay loader. Zenas escaped from death to life a third time at the age of eight, when his father led him to saving faith in the Lord Jesus Christ, this in the very same room where he had originally been declared dead as a newborn baby.

Considering what Dr. Gerig accomplished and the length of his days, his story is evidence that purpose cannot die. It shows the hand of God in his life from an early age and tells us the source of the flame in his heart to make a difference in the world. No wonder in founding his first school for higher Christian education, the Jamaica Theological Seminary (JTS), the motto was, "That I might know Him, that I might preach Him". This God-story should lift our faith every time it is told. If you are floundering in faith or believing God for a miracle, may this story renew your faith, hope and trust in the God who makes the impossible possible.

Dr. Zenas E. Gerig was born on February 27, 1927, on a farm near Spencerville, Indiana. He died at age 84 on September 14, 2011 in Lowell, Indiana. After high school Dr. Gerig earned a B.A. from Ft. Wayne Bible College.

He married his "brown-eyed sweetheart", Esther Lehman, on June 12, 1952 and in 1954, he was ordained as a minister by the Missionary Church. Their first son, Stephen, was born in New York. Their second child Laurel was born in Jamaica, and Stan was born during a furlough in the USA. At the time of Dr. Gerig's passing, he had nine grandchildren.

While serving in Jamaica, he earned a Master of Divinity from New York Theological Seminary, a Master of Science and Doctor of Philosophy in Education from Indiana University.

He, with his wife Esther, served for 43 years in Jamaica with the Overseas Board of the Missionary Church, Inc. He first served as a pastor and then as an educator. As an educator, he founded two theological institutions of higher learning: the bachelors level Jamaica Theological Seminary in 1960, and the master's level Caribbean Graduate School of Theology in 1986.

During his missionary sojourn in Jamaica, he served with multiple Jamaican, Caribbean and international organizations involving Christian higher education and the evangelical churches. There were 46 articles in the Jamaica Gleaner Archives which captured Dr. Gerig's involvement in the nation's life from as early June 15, 1959. They spoke to the progress of the two schools he founded, and his service to the Jamaica Association of Evangelicals (JAE), now known as Jamaica Evangelical Alliance. One article dated June 27, 1981, listed him as a member-at-large and representative of the Missionary Church Association in Jamaica.

The Fire to Serve

Dr. Zenas Gerig and his wife, Esther, left their comfort zone in the United States and arrived in Jamaica in 1954. Shirley Ham of KPM News in Kendallville, Indiana interviewed the Gerigs in 2001. Her interview captured the couple's perspective of their service in Jamaica. In this article, Dr. Gerig provided this rationale for his service in Jamaica. "I had made a commitment to the Lord that I would go anywhere he would lead, and he led there."

This commitment led him to Jamaica, where he began his service as the pastor of Emmanuel Missionary Church in Mandeville. There he served for three years before moving to Kingston to lead the efforts in higher Christian education. According to Dr. Gerig,

> It wasn't long before we realized that they (the nationals) were more cut out for the work than I was. I got down there and discovered I needed more education if I was going to be in education. The only problem was, there was no school [*no suitable theological institute*]. Although there were about 50 Bible institutes, none compared to the post-high-school bachelor level of the U.S.

Note: The insertion in parenthesis is that of the author for clarity.

When the couple decided to leave the pastorate and start a school, the Overseas Board of the Missionary Church asked them to move from Mandeville to start their efforts in Kingston. The move to Kingston posed some climatic challenges. Mrs. Gerig at first had trouble with the heat. Ms. Ham reports that "One time she even collapsed and had to be rushed to the hospital." Mandeville being located some 2000 feet above sea level (known as "cool cool Mandeville" to many Jamaicans) was manageable compared to Kingston.

They however weathered the challenges, and in the sixth year of their mission in Jamaica, they started the Caribbean's first theological seminary, the Jamaica Theological Seminary. The Gerigs started the school in their home with four full-time students after contacting high school students who were heading out to college abroad. They wanted to offer the same quality theological education locally. For the next decade there were no more than 13 students, but the Gerigs persevered, being faithful to their call.

Dr. Gerig noted, "We wanted more, but we took who the Lord sent." Since Dr. Gerig was conscious of the need for quality standards in higher Christian education, and JTS needed credibility, the couple set their own standards. Later Dr. Gerig met with educators in London, Africa, Europe and all over the Caribbean in an effort to ensure JTS's programmes were of the standard to be accredited. The Jamaican government had not yet established a quality assurance system for tertiary education in Jamaica.

Note: The Gerig's work started in Jamaica before Jamaica's independence, and continued when the country was in its early stage of development as an independent nation.

In his efforts to ensure that JTS was meeting the quality assurance standards for tertiary institutions, Dr. Gerig visited 52 countries, some of which had accreditation systems for theological education at the tertiary level.

Dr. Gerig explained in his interview with Ms. Ham, "By the time the International Council of Accreditation Agency was finished with their examination, they commended us. The college (JTS) proved to be a resounding success." Mrs. Gerig noted, "We saw our first graduates come out as key leaders in the para-churches, so we felt it was worth it... It's interesting to stay in something long enough to see it bear fruit."

The tremendous work done by Dr Gerig in ensuring quality standards in theological education at the tertiary level, explains why JTS was ready for evaluation by the University Council of Jamaica (UCJ) which was established in 1987 as the national external quality assurance body for tertiary education. JTS was the first institution to have been registered by the UCJ, and to have had a programme accredited. The institution was registered and the then Bachelor of Theology was accredited in 1991.

Dr. Gerig led JTS as principal for 25 years. After the success of JTS, the Gerigs did not stop there. Dr. Gerig was still concerned about the brain drain in Jamaica with the flow of the country's best minds to other countries for higher education, then a career.

Furthermore, the Caribbean Evangelical Theological Association (CETA) saw the need for a regional Graduate School of Theology to serve the evangelical churches of the region. This led to the decision of CETA to establish a Graduate School. Dr. Gerig, one of the founding officials of CETA, was appointed to lead the project to establish the

Caribbean Graduate School of Theology. He then led CGST as its President from 1987-1992.

Dr. Palmer (2002) in his tribute in CJET noted that while Dr. Gerig was arranging for others' education, he postponed his own. He returned to the US every other summer, completed deputation work, reported on the progress in churches and collected library books by the hundreds. Perhaps this explains why the schools named the library (The Zenas Gerig Library) after him.

After 13 years, he received his master's degree and doctorate in education at Indiana University. The focus of his doctoral research (completed in 1977) was adult education and the church, "an area which he felt held promise in playing a crucial role in the development of the new Jamaica" (CJET, June 2002). It is instructive that his life's work was closely connected with his studies and his legacy.

Honoured for Serving

A Jamaica Gleaner feature on June 20, 2010, captured the nation's appreciation for the service of Dr. Zenas Gerig to the development of Jamaica, referring to the honour bestowed on him by the government of Jamaica in 2001.

The government conferred on him the Order of Distinction in the honorary rank of Commander (CD) at the National Heroes' Day Awards Ceremony. This honour was conferred on him in recognition of his work as founder of the two schools, the Jamaica Theological Seminary and the Caribbean Graduate School of Theology. This award is Jamaica's fifth highest national honour. The government also recognized Dr. Gerig for his service as a leader in the Missionary Church in Jamaica and the evangelical community worldwide. Prior to this award, the CGST had conferred on him in 2001, a Doctor of Divinity honoris causa for his service in education.

The flame of service and commitment to follow God wherever he leads has borne much fruit. We can learn many lessons from this brief retelling of the life and legacy of Dr. Gerig. Chief among these lessons is: the need to be faithful to the call since faithfulness has its rewards.

These honours are even more significant considering the information shared by his son, Stan Gerig, that there were some who had doubted he was the right man for the job. But Dr. Gerig never let the doubters stop him and his work now speaks for itself.

When he died in 2011, the magnitude of the tributes from those who knew him, from students and from graduates of his schools further vindicated him, proving that he had been the right man for the job.

Stories of Impact

I have been a beneficiary of Dr. Gerig's flame for much longer than I realized. My pastor was trained at the JTS and is a former CGST student. JTS is the chief training arm for ministers in the Missionary Church Association in Jamaica. For many years, without this training, you could not become a pastor in the Missionary Church. It was he who convinced me to attend JTS when I was contemplating attending an overseas university.

My pastor proudly mentioned the fact that JTS had accredited programmes, and therefore I had no need to fear attending the institution. So, I did. I entered JTS, the first institution Dr. Gerig founded, at the young age of 21, and I did not know where the path would lead, but I knew it was a place that would equip me for ministry.

Within a year of graduating from JTS, I began investigating the possibility of matriculating to Yale University. One day, Dr. Dameon Black, one of my lecturers, then Acting President of JTS and a graduate of CGST, redirected me to CGST. He even offered to pay for my first course. In fact, he directed me to a particular programme (and told me to do it) which he recommended I pursue because he believed I could write. So, I did—just as I had done with my pastor's recommendation.

At CGST, I pursued the Master of Arts in Theological Studies with an emphasis on Intercultural Studies. Thus, I attended both of the institutions founded by Dr. Gerig and became a beneficiary of his work. Today my current network is 80% related to both institutions. Through JTS I found my best friends, and through CGST I found some of my best mentors. Had these graduates not been impacted by Dr. Gerig's flame, my life would have been completely different.

My experiences are not unique. The flame of transformation continues to burn at CGST and JTS. There are many graduate stories that tell of the impact of these two guardians of Dr. Gerig's flame. Their graduates are carriers of the flame.

Tributes in Death (September 2011)

These are some tributes paid to Dr. Gerig by students, graduates and colleagues at his passing. They capture his life, impact and legacy. They were posted on the website, Legacy.com, in Grand Rapids, Michigan.

Dr. Gerig was a Christian gentleman and a pioneer missionary educator in the Caribbean, a founder of leading schools of theology. That work is a legacy that will live on in the solidity it has provided to the Evangelical Christian faith in our region. May our Risen Lord comfort the bereaved, and may we all draw inspiration from his legacy.

—Gordon Mullings

My outstanding memory of Dr. Gerig is that he was a servant leader. There was nothing too insignificant for him to do, and he empowered those with whom he worked so that we could give of our best. I was impressed by his unwavering faith, his faithfulness and his optimism. He was the ultimate eternal optimist. As a result, he has left a rich and enduring legacy to the education of Christian leaders in the Caribbean.

—Dr. Claire Henry

Pastor Gerig baptized my sisters and myself in 1957. He was our first pastor and I cannot forget how he instructed us for baptism. He gave us a sound teaching in Christian living. He loved the young people and faithfully taught us the word. He was a devout leader and an example of a true saint of God. His life was truly dedicated to God, and he will always be remembered. My love and prayers are with his blessed family

—Sandra and Joan Reynolds, NY

Condolences to Mrs. Gerig and the family of the late Dr. Zenas Gerig. He has left a legacy in Jamaica which will remain until Christ returns. He was a leader who led by example earnest, humble, hardworking, a visionary who invested in the lives of persons for continuity of the spread of the word of God and the building of His CHURCH.

—Mary Clarke

Dr. Gerig was an authentic Christian with a very generous heart and immense compassion. His missionary work and vision have anchored the Missionary Church and left an indelible Christian footprint in the island of Jamaica. I will never forget your kindness to me in Jamaica.

— Sammy Jagarnauth, New York

Dr. Zenas Gerig was a visionary educator. He has left a rich legacy that will persist for many years to come. His legacy lives on through the institutions he founded including the Jamaica Theological Seminary (JTS) and the Caribbean Graduate School of Theology (CGST). His legacy lives on in the work of the Caribbean Evangelical Theological Association (CETA) that he helped to found.

His legacy lives on also through the accreditation service which he pioneered through CETA. Moreover, his legacy lives on in and through the lives and ministries of those of us who have been the beneficiaries of the institutions and services he pioneered.

—Rev. Dr. Errol Joseph, JTS 1986, CGST 1992;
& Mrs. Lorrien Joseph, JTS 1992

My opinion of Brother Zenas Gerig is that he was a devoted and dedicated servant of the Lord. He was a role model for any young man that aspired to be an authentic human being. I will always remember him with respect as a hero of faith. (I am a graduate of JTS, 1964)

—Ransford Nicholson

Condolences to the family and friends of Dr. Zenas Gerig, a man who had a FULL life not because of the quantity of years he lived, but because of the quality; he fulfilled his God-given purpose! He allowed God to build a foundation in him and laid the foundation at JTS which has been the equipping station for so many church leaders.

—Ricardo Piper

'The final test of a leader is that he leaves behind in others the conviction and will to carry on' (Walter Lippman). Dr. Zenas Gerig has amply demonstrated this and left behind a legacy to the Caribbean Church in trained Christian leaders. Only eternity will reveal the full impact of his sacrificial labours!

—Dr. Orville Neil

Dr. Zenas Gerig was a man of vision. The many students and the sturdy buildings of the much-expanded campus are testimony to that fact. He saw what most Christian leaders in Jamaica never saw at the time of his arrival from Indiana.

In my mind are pictures and incidents still fresh as he sought to initiate his vision practically. There were many things to discourage. But with faith firm in Christ and for His cause he pressed on to the glory of God.

—Billy Hall

Dr. Zenas Gerig was for me one of God's great and very special servants. His gentleness of spirit, his vision for developing Christian leadership excellence across the Caribbean, his perseverance in achieving this vision, and the quality of his personal life have left a legacy that will continue to impact future generations. He was someone I admired deeply and thank God for the impact of his witness on my life and ministry.

—Gerry Gallimore

Thank you for giving to the Lord, I am a life that was changed. May the abiding presence of God be with the family of Dr. Gerig.

—Brent James

Dr. Gerig, a humble giant who walked on the campus of Jamaica Theological Seminary with purpose and focus. I will always remember him quietly going about his tasks and a smile on his face.

—Rev. Ronald Webster

In reading these tributes, one cannot help but feel inspired. It is simply wonderful to see how this Christian clergyman chose a path of transformation and service that went beyond the precincts of his local church, native country and home.

It is evidence of a beneficial cross-cultural partnership which has empowered the Caribbean. Dr. Gerig was faithful to the call of God, amidst challenges and it has borne lasting fruit. The flame of transformation shone brightly in the tributes. He was truly a transformational leader par excellence. The schools he founded must continue as the guardians of this flame and keep it blazing.

His son, Stan Gerig is the Acting Chairman of the Board of Governors for CGST. Dr. Gerig believed in higher education for Christian leaders as a key to expanding God's kingdom. He showed this in his own life. He was committed to faithful service within and beyond the four walls of the church with training in areas relevant to society's needs.

Dr. Gerig worked diligently to ensure the programs in his schools gained accreditation. He was committed to excellent standards in theological education at the tertiary level. He wanted the graduates to be unhindered in their educational pursuits elsewhere, and to be qualified to serve and lead in different fields as ambassadors for Christ. Their excellent training would help them create relationships to make Christ known, as Christ was the source of the flame which burnt brightly in Dr. Gerig's heart.

Part II:

CGST: A Guardian of the Flame

3.

Equipping "The Called"

"…And the things you have heard me say in the presence of many witnesses entrust to reliable men who will also be qualified to teach others" —2 Timothy 2:2, NIV

The leader who does not raise up a successor has failed, and our Lord Jesus left a masterful example. When He departed the earthly scene, Jesus left 12 apostles as chief leaders and a company of disciples from which they could choose other leaders in case one of those apostles failed. Jesus ensured the mission continued after Him, and so did Dr. Gerig.

Dr. Gerig's vision of raising up indigenous Caribbean leaders has been clearly demonstrated in those who succeeded him in the leadership of the institutions he founded. He led CGST for five years (1987-1992). After him, Dr. Dieumeme Noelliste of Haiti was the first indigenous president (1992-2007). Dr. Las Newman of Jamaica served as the second President of CGST (2008–2013). Dr. John Keane of Jamaica served as Acting President from 2013 until Dr. David Corbin of Trinidad was appointed as President (2017–2020), and today the institution is led by its first female President Dr. Viviene Kerr of Jamaica (2020–present).

In 1992, Dr. Roger Ringenberg wrote an extensive dissertation on the history of JTS and included the formation of CGST and its progress up to 1992 in partial completion for his doctorate of Missiology degree. The sister schools had the same founder. They share campuses and had shared administration until 2004. One cannot write about one without mentioning the other.

In doing the research for this book, I found several articles in the Jamaican newspapers which captured the history and progress of CGST. For example, an article in 2011 in the Jamaica Gleaner in commemoration of CGST's 25th anniversary, comprehensively chronicled the history and growth of CGST 1986-2011. Yet again, at the installation of its second indigenous president, Dr. Las Newman, there was an article about CGST and in 2020, at the installation of its first female president, CGST again took centre stage in Jamaica's two leading newspapers (Jamaica Gleaner and the Jamaica Observer).

In this section of the book, some of this information is repeated but curtailed. For a more extensive read, you can explore these resources listed in the reference section of the book. Since this book is a short inspirational read, this chapter summarizes the school, its programs and achievements over the years, along with stories of impact.

A Beacon of Higher Education

CGST is nestled in the heart of the city of Kingston, at 18-20 West Avenue in Constant Spring (Kingston 8), approximately five minutes away from the Half-Way Tree Transport Center. It has been a beacon of higher Christian education since it began operations in 1986. The school officially opened on the 8th of September with 20 students; 12 part-time and 8 full-time. It uses a modular method of programme delivery, with courses delivered in intensive three-week modules. The academic year is September through to June.

According to Ringenburg's "A History of Jamaica Theological Seminary 1960-1992," the World Evangelical Fellowship Global Report stated that CGST had accomplished two firsts. It was the first seminary in the Caribbean offering graduate level training and its modular approach was the first of its kind in the Caribbean (1992, p. 214). CGST was established under the sponsorship of the Caribbean Evangelical Theological Association (CETA), a consortium of some 50 under-graduate theological institutions scattered throughout the Caribbean region and belonging to various church groups.

CGST's mission, vision and passion outlined on its website clearly capture the Gerig flame. Its mission is to provide Christians with quality and Christ-centered graduate level training, for the strengthening of the church, the transformation of society in the Caribbean and beyond, for the glory of God.

CGST's vision is to produce an ever-increasing number of godly men and women, deployed in the Caribbean and beyond who will have a transforming impact in church and society.

Its passion is to have a transforming impact on church and society by providing a teaching/learning experience that integrates biblical principles and academic excellence.

As a graduate school with programmes accredited by CETA and the University Council of Jamaica, CGST operates interdenominationally and stresses commitment to the Christian worldview, academic excellence, contextual relevance, spiritual sensitivity and practical involvement. Its purpose is to take part in shaping the future of the Caribbean by training men and women who have a passion to change our region for the better by the application of biblical principles to professional life.

In its 35-year history (1986-2021), the CGST has trained over 700 hundred graduates who are currently serving across the length and breadth of the Caribbean. CGST's ministry also reaches beyond the Caribbean region to such places as the United States, Canada, the United Kingdom and Africa.

Like its founder, many of CGST's graduates attain terminal degrees. They occupy key leadership positions in the church and carry out their work in the secular domain. These include working in the media, the civil service, school system, government, correctional services, law enforcement, law, business and book publishing.

Still, others are responding to the crises facing the youth and families in our society through the counselling ministry in schools and many social agencies. Some, like

Dr. Gerig, lead and serve in institutions of higher learning for their denominations and with accreditation bodies like CETA. These disciples of Gerig carry his imprint. They keep his flame burning brightly.

CGST's Programmes and Achievements

CGST has a rich history. On June 16, 1989, CGST held its first graduation service jointly with JTS at Grace Missionary Church. On that occasion 8 of the initial 20 enrolled students graduated with master's degrees in three disciplines. They were as follows:

M.A. in Biblical Studies
Andy Owen Homer (Hons)
Delano Vincent Palmer

M.A. in Christian Education
Lester Ferguson

M.A. in Counselling Psychology
Faith Thomas (Hons)
David McLean
Maria Vassell (Hons)
Reslyn Simmonds
Angela Ramlal-Williams (Hons)

According to Ringenburg (1992), in the opening year, CGST offered two degrees: Master of Arts in Biblical Studies and the Master of Arts in Christian Education. The following year in 1987, they added a Master of Arts in

Counselling Psychology. Between 1986 and December 2021, CGST has offered eight graduate training programs.

Master of Arts in Christian Education
Master of Arts in Caribbean Ministries
Master of Arts in Interdisciplinary Studies
Master of Arts in Theological Studies
Master of Arts in Counselling Psychology
Master of Divinity
Master of Business Administration (MBA
Doctor of Ministry

The Master of Arts in Caribbean Ministries was a two-year interdisciplinary programme which allowed for an emphasis in either Missions, Christian Education, or Counselling Psychology. This along with the M.A. in Christian education became the M.A. in Interdisciplinary Studies.

The Master of Arts in Theological Studies, which I pursued, provides for a concentration in either Biblical Studies, Theological Studies, or Missions (Intercultural Studies). The Master of Arts in Counselling Psychology is a specialized degree for those desiring skills in counselling and interpersonal relations. It acquaints students with the data and theories of psychology, which are applicable to a healing ministry both in the Church and in society at large.

The Master of Divinity provides for a three-year programme of study for students who need training for a career in professional ministry. In 2006, the school launched a Master of Business Administration (MBA) degree and in 2010, a doctoral programme (DMin) in partnership with Bakke Graduate University, Seattle, Washington. This is the school at which I am currently pursuing a doctoral programme in Transformational Leadership.

For many years in its early development, CGST partnered with Dr. Barry Davidson (CD) of family life ministries to offer counselling services. Dr. Davidson served as the Director of the Psychology programme and was part of the resident teaching staff.

Today the school has significantly scaled down its programmes and operations, and is facing serious financial challenges. As of January 2021, only two of its early degrees are being offered: Master of Arts in Theological Studies and Master of Arts in Counselling Psychology as its core training programmes.

In sharing Dr. Gerig's story and those of its graduates, highlighting the impact of the school, we hope there will be a revival and expansion of CGST's training programmes in the near future.

Over the years, many outstanding evangelical scholars from the Caribbean region and international circles have assisted in teaching courses at CGST as visiting lecturers. These include Old Testament Scholar, Dr. Walter Kaiser (USA); Aida Besancon Spencer (Dominican Republic); Dr. Gleason Archer (USA); Dr. Gary Collins (Canada); Dr. Herbert Jacobson (USA); Dr. Stanton Jones (USA); Dr. Richard Longnecker (Canada) and Dr. Ronald F. Youngblood (Canada).

The school has conferred 28 honorary doctoral degrees (1993-2020) on regional and international persons who have demonstrated distinguished service and exemplary Christian scholarship to the broader Caribbean society. The recipients are listed below.

Rex Major	1993	Bahamas
Gerald Gallimore	1994	Jamaica
Edner Jenty	1995	Haiti
Wingrove Taylor	1996	Barbados
Cleveland Grant	1997	Jamaica
David Carlson	1998	USA
Faith Linton	1999	Jamaica
Alister Alexander	2000	Trinidad & Tobago
Zenas Gerig	2001	USA
Roberto Rivera	2002	Puerto Rico
Gerald Seale	2004	Barbados
Clinton Chisholm	2005	Jamaica
Joel Edwards	2006	Jamaica/England
Jean Duthene Joseph	2007	Haiti
Carlton Cumberbatch	2008	Barbados
David Baer	2008	USA
Peter Spencer	2010	Jamaica
Cecelia Spencer	2010	Jamaica
Lindsay Brown	2011	England/Wales
Neville Callam	2011	Jamaica
Frank Goveia	2012	Guyana/England
Burchell Taylor	2013	Jamaica
Alfred Sangster	2013	Jamaica
Lenworth Anglin	2014	Jamaica
Ruby Thompson	2017	Trinidad & Tobago
Lloyd Cooke	2018	Jamaica
Everard Allen	2019	Jamaica
Joan Pinkney	2020	Jamaica

In 2009, CGST appointed the following distinguished fellows as Scholar Ambassadors: the Rev. Canon Dr. Joel

Edwards, DD., DL. (International Christian Mission leader); Professor Brendan C. Bain, D.M., Professor of Public Health, University of the West Indies; Dr. Barry A. Wade, PhD., OD, ecologist and Christian engagement specialist; Dr. Henley W. Morgan, PhD, business consultant, public educator, and Christian leader, as part of efforts to strengthen the church in the region.

Even without an appointment, each graduate is automatically an ambassador for CGST, and the work of CGST's graduates strengthens the effort of the church in the region and beyond. When graduates share their experiences or invite others to enroll in the school, they automatically become carriers of the Gerig flame, and contribute to the growth of CGST.

As we close this section, note carefully what four recent graduates (2020) had to say about their experience and CGST's impact on them. We hope that as a result of reading their testimonies, you too will become part of the CGST family and help in its expansion.

2020 Graduate Stories of Impact

Graduate: Candice Reynolds
Programme: Masters of Arts in Theological Studies
Country: Jamaica

The Masters of Arts in Theological Studies programme, at CGST is multifaceted. It exposed me to dimensions of theology that I had not been aware of before. I appreciated the wealth of knowledge imparted to me by my lecturers. Their guidance, expertise and support helped me to comfortably complete my programme excellently.

During the programme my faith was challenged in ways it had not been challenged before. I had to put aside my own presuppositions about theology and study it objectively. This exercise, though uncomfortable at times, allowed my faith to grow in new areas.

CGST unlocked potential that I did not realize I had. For example, various lecturers would commend me on several papers I presented. This was encouraging and boosted my confidence to write research papers. There were times during the programme when I wanted to stop because of challenges but the encouragement, and support, of the lecturers, staff and students helped me to persevere to the end.

Studying at CGST has positively impacted my life because it was not solely about rigorous academics. It was more about transformational and Christ-centered learning. The lecturers, staff and students were like family. Although studying was a challenge in this period, the family-centered environment was conducive to an enjoyable experience.

Note: Candice also served as a member CGST's administrative staff and was part of the CGST team that worked with me to make this book a reality. Thank you, Candice.

Graduate: Lisa Renee Wilson-Gittens
Programme: Master of Arts in Theological Studies
Country: Saint Maarten

I have had my shares of highs, lows and bends in the road during my time at CGST. When things were thorny—personally, spiritually or academically, the godly men and women were quick to step in as caring counsellors, praying intercessors and advisors. It is a blessing to be greeted in class with devotionals or have a telephone call to administration during which professionals freely share their faith.

Over the many years of my time with CGST, the presidents, deans, teaching and administrative staff have been supportive of my journey and willing to assist a distant-learner who was following face-to-face classes online in innovative ways.

During my internship, the COVID-19 pandemic levelled the playing field as all churches in both Jamaica and Saint Maarten were ordered to suspend congregational meetings in a shared space. CGST made it possible for me to serve a Jamaican-based ministry online, though living in Saint Maarten. I thank YHWH for His promise, the process and my purpose, and the role CGST played in it… 'I am confident in this, He who has begun a good work in you [and me] shall perfect it...' (Philippians 1:6).

Graduate: Ricardo Lee (Valedictorian)
Programme: Master of Arts in Counselling Psychology
Country: Jamaica

This programme has really enhanced my capacity at work and has benefited me otherwise. I would definitely recommend it to anyone who would like to develop intellectual acumen while paying attention to spiritual growth. Also, for persons who would like to integrate Psychology with Theology, this institution is definitely here for you.

Since I've been at CGST, I have experienced increases in my spiritual maturity and have seen overall improvement as a whole person. The staff is warm. They are student-centered. You can speak to them about your challenges and they are always responsive. As you pursue your studies, CGST makes it almost as easy as 123, just because of the kind of environment created by students and staff who fit in with shared values. CGST is my institution and I would recommend this institution for graduate training to everyone.

·   ·   ·   ·   ·

Graduate: Fay Robinson-Tee
Programme: Master of Arts in Counselling Psychology
Country: Jamaica

Fay shared her testimony of impact creatively through a poem, "CGST Made Me."

I learnt to care, empathy share…CGST MADE ME.
Balance life's tasks; home, work, school, church …CGST MADE ME.

With poise and dignity to stand, express self as an academician…CGST MADE ME!

Enriched in spirituality; love, faith, trust, live pure heartedly…CGST MADE ME!

The journey long, has now ended, equipped to face the next challenge…CGST MADE ME!

Now to the world I go, 'IBLESS', standing on six basic tenets…CGST GAVE ME!!

Integrity, Biblical view, Love, Excellence, Servanthood too… CGST TAUGHT ME!!

The quiver holds one arrow yet; Spiritual formation, so in-depth…CGST SHAPED ME!!

My story is true, I'll tell it well. New students to this path propel. This little giant…great indeed, germinated from a simple seed. But nourished in the soil of faith…expand, stay strong, you're anchored deep.

May these stories of impact inspire you. May you catch the flame like I did, and partner with CGST to maintain the vision and legacy of Dr. Zenas Gerig.

Part III:

Carriers of the Flame
Outstanding Graduates
1989-2009

CGST's Outstanding Flame Carriers

"So I urge you, be imitators of me [just as a child imitates his father]."—1 Corinthians 4:16, AMP

In the same way your children carry your genes and their physical features mirror yours, so it has been with many graduates of the schools Dr. Gerig founded. These flame carriers bear his imprint. In reading the profiles and testimonies of these outstanding graduates, you will see that almost all have attained terminal degrees. They are all leading in their fields and have served the church and their nation well.

Some became principals of schools like Dr. Gerig did, and some are even involved in the accreditation of programmes for theological education. One of them created history at CGST by becoming the first female president of the institution in June 2020. But how did we choose 12 graduates from over 700, when so many have done outstanding work in the Caribbean?

After making the book proposal to Dr. David Corbin, then president of CGST, about partnering with CGST, he and his team spearheaded the efforts to identify the list of outstanding graduates. Although initial discussions about the book began under Dr. Corbin's leadership, it was the new President, Dr. Viviene Kerr, who officially signed off on the proposal and led the efforts to complete the criteria for selection of the list of graduates.

It was very difficult to shortlist the names of outstanding graduates over the first 20 years. From a list of 30 candidates, we shortlisted it to 12 graduates. Dr. Kerr along with two members of her staff sent letters to the candidates explaining the vision and inviting them to share their stories. I followed up and from the number of graduates contacted; we chose the first 12 who responded.

Perhaps in later years and other volumes, CGST can showcase the others. We are grateful for the positive responses of these graduates and their permission to share their profiles in this book. See below, the criteria for selection and the names of these outstanding graduates.

Selection Criteria

- Christian Leaders with a record of significant impact over the past 20 years
- Graduates of any programme offered since the inception of institution
- Gender balance—mixture of male and female
- Cohorts from 1989 to 2009
- Commitment to God and purpose

- Known for not compromising their Christian principles and moral standards
- Possess high standards of integrity
- Made/making remarkable and tangible contributions to their field of study or sphere of influence through creating life-changing interventions and programmes that would have impacted lives positively (This can be as part of an organisation or self-employed)- within their own country and the Caribbean
- Evidence of consistency
- Must be able to show how being a student at the Caribbean Graduate School of Theology would have significantly impacted their success
- Evidence of giving back in a small or large way to community and/or society
- Responsiveness to the request from CGST to share their stories (during the given timeline).

The names of the featured graduates, programme of study, country of origin and year of graduation are listed as follows:

1. Dr. Delano Vincent Palmer, M.A. in Biblical Studies, Jamaica, 1989
2. Mrs. Faith Thomas, M.A. in Counselling Psychology, Jamaica, 1989
3. Dr. Errol Joseph, M.A. in Christian Education, Trinidad, 1991
4. Dr. Anthony Oliver, M.A. in Biblical Studies, Trinidad, 1991

5. Ms. Erica Campbell, M.A. in Caribbean Ministries & Master of Divinity, Jamaica, 1994 & 1996

6. Dr. Rawle Tyson, M.A. in Caribbean Ministries, Jamaica, 1995

7. Dr. Viviene Kerr, M.A. in Counselling Psychology, Jamaica, 2000

8. Dr. Joan Pinkney, M.A. in Counselling Psychology, Jamaica, 2001

9. Dr. Earlmont Williams, M.A. in Intercultural Studies & Master of Divinity, St Vincent and the Grenadines, 2002 & 2006

10. Rev. Courtney Stewart, Master of Business Administration, Jamaica, 2008

11. Dr. Yvette Stupart, M.A. in Counselling Psychology, Jamaica, 2000

12. Mrs. Pat Eves McKenzie, M.A. in Counselling Psychology, Jamaica, 1996

From their profiles, you will get a sense of the transformational impact of CGST and, by extension, that of Dr. Gerig. You will also find hope and inspiration to pursue your God-given mission, despite the odds.

Graduate Feature Questions

We asked the outstanding graduates to respond to the following questions, along with providing a professional profile and brief biography.

1. What are your current responsibilities professionally and ministry wise?

2. What would you say has been your greatest contribution to society and or the kingdom of God over the years? [Don't be shy]

3. Have you received any professional, ministry, national or regional awards? If so, name them.

4. When did you graduate from CGST and why did you attend CGST?

5. What were your greatest challenges as a student, and how did you overcome them? [Name 1-3]

6. How has CGST impacted your life, ministry and career?

7. How has the life of Zenas Gerig impacted you?

8. What would be your number one advice to prospective students?

9. Why would you encourage them to study at CGST?

May their stories, achievements and responses inspire you to serve God with unswerving commitment, attain Christian education at the highest level, become part of the CGST family and play your part in advancing the welfare of the kingdom and the region. We have dubbed them GGST Flame Carriers to inspire you to also become a flame carrier.

CGST Flame Carrier
Dr. Delano Palmer

Graduation: 1989, M.A. in Biblical Studies (Hons.)
Career: Author, NT Scholar and Bible Teacher
Birth: August 18, 1951
Birthplace: Jamaica
Married: Dotty Palmer
Children: Two Adult Children;
Grandchildren: One

Dr. **Delano Palmer** is one of the first graduates of CGST and the valedictorian of that batch. He is an author, New Testament scholar, former Deputy Vice President of the Jamaica Theological Seminary, adjunct lecturer at CGST, and former scholar in residence. He has a tremendous sense of humor and this comes out in his testimonial and Q and A.

He's a proud member of CAFU (Christian Ambassadors Footballers United), as well as a former player with Cavalier and Santos, all of which he represented on winning teams. He was born the very day after Marcus Garvey's birthday and hurricane Charlie.

His Testimony

In Dr. Palmer's late teens, he went to St Elizabeth Technical High School on a football scholarship. While at this school, he became a Christian. Below is his testimony.

I can recall quite vividly the worst day of my life. It was also one of the worst days in the annals of Jamaica's history (Kendal crash). It was a day of destruction and death. It is by God's mercy why I am still alive, and that I did not perish with the scores of others who did.

That day, though a very sad one, has also helped me to appreciate the best day of my life—a day that was also integrally connected with the grace and mercy of God. Long before that special day, I took a very serious view of life, struggling hard throughout my teen years to be upright and decent. I tried to be a Christian, but the harder I tried, the greater my failure seemed.

While attending St Elizabeth Technical High School (STETHS), I was reading a book about health and longevity which emphasized the importance of keeping God's law. I began trying to obey by not drinking, maintaining sexual purity, and by keeping the other areas of God's law. But the more I tried, the more I failed. I became miserable and frustrated.

One day I came across a copy of the "Caribbean Challenge," a regional monthly at the time, and read all the way through it. The path of salvation was simply presented in a way I had not seen before. And then that day came: the happiest day of my life.

One evening, conscious of failure and feeling miserable, I came under strong conviction of my need for Christ. My efforts at personal reformation having failed, I shared with my girlfriend my desire to trust Christ and Him alone for salvation. My friend was interested but was not ready to make that kind of commitment.

I decided to go it alone. I left the roadway, knelt in the bushes and cried to the Lord for salvation. When I rose from my knees, my friend was praying nearby. Both of us accepted Christ as our personal Saviour that memorable Thursday in November 1970.

The following Sunday we went together to the (Rose of) Sharon Baptist Church in Santa Cruz. What really happened to us then? A promise we had claimed was fulfilled. The Bible affirms that whoever calls on the name of the Lord will be delivered (Romans 10:13). On that day we were delivered from a future of total alienation from God's presence, from the guilt of our past, and from the misery of a hopeless present. Put another way, we were guaranteed a brighter tomorrow and a meaningful today, with all God's power at our disposal—and all of this courtesy of the life and work of Christ Jesus on the Santa Cruz (Holy Cross). He was the One who died that we might live; He is the One coming again so that we might live forever.

Since his salvific experience over many years, Dr. Palmer has pursued higher education vigorously. He gained a diploma in Theology from Midland Bible Institute; a bachelor's degree from Carver College in Atlanta, USA, a master's degree at CGST; a Masters in Religious Education from Cornerstone University in Grand Rapids, Michigan, U.S.A, and his terminal degree, a Doctor of Theology from the University of South Africa in Pretoria.

He is the author of several journal articles, the latest of which is "Sam Sharpe and the Future of Caribbean Theology," *CJET* 20 (2021): 43-58. His recent books include *New Testament Theology: Identity and I-deology* (2019) and *Acts: A Contextual Commentary* (2020). He is a member of several professional organizations:

- Theological Commission, Caribbean Evange-lical Theological Association (2001- present)
- Society of Biblical Literature (2006-2008; 2016; 2018-present)
- Society of Caribbean Professors of Religious Studies (2017-present)

- Studiorum Novi Testamenti Societas, SNTS (2015-present)

GRADUATE Q and A

Q. What are your current responsibilities professsionally and ministry wise?

A. I am a member of Swallowfield Chapel where I serve as a Bible Teacher in the Adult Christian Education programme (ACE) and Adjunct lecturer at CGST and JTS. I served as Academic Dean at JTS from 2009-2013, until I was promoted to Deputy President. My tenure as Deputy President ended in 2016.

Q. What would you say has been your greatest contribution to society and or the kingdom of God over the years?

A. Serving on the team that translated the New Testament into the best language since sliced bread (Jamaican also known as Patois). Being a part of the teams at CGST and JTS preparing scores of persons serving all over the globe promoting human flourishing.

Q. What were your greatest challenges as a student and how did you overcome them? [Name 1-3]

A. Working and studying. Doing (concurrently) a Masters of Religious Education at Cornerstone University, since it was accredited. At CGST two years of study were promised; at the end of the second year, an additional year was added to write a thesis (*mi did bex*!). It turned out to be a blessing in disguise!

Q. How has CGST impacted your life, ministry or career?

A. Having majored in Biblical Studies/Theology and minored in Counselling Psychology, the impact, under God, is incalculable.

Q. How has the life of Zenas Gerig impacted you?

A. He was the one who recruited and gave me a scholarship to attend CGST. I was blessed greatly by his ministry and registered my gratitude in a written tribute. Dr. Gerig has made a significant contribution to nation building, and his doctoral dissertation (among other things too numerous to mention) is a signal testimony to that fact.

Q. What would be your number one advice to prospective students?

A. Take the following gems quite seriously: The unexamined life is not worth living (Socrates); as well as I Thessalonians 5: 21, by the apostle Paul, "but test them all; hold on to what is good."

Q. Why would you encourage them to study at CGST?

A. Both programmes are rigorous and rewarding and spiritually refreshing.

CGST FLAME CARRIER
Mrs. Faith Marie Thomas

Graduation: 1989, M.A in Counselling Psychology
Career: Counselling Psychologist and Educator
Birth: July 26, 1958
Country of Origin: Jamaica
First of three children
Married: Dr. Donovan Thomas, 1986
Children: Two—Daniel and Joseph (both married)
Grandchildren: One

Mrs. *Faith Thomas,* like Dr. Delano Palmer, had the privilege of being one of the first graduates of CGST. She is an author, Counselling Psychologist and Vice President and co-founder of Choose Life International, a ministry she and her husband Dr. Donovan Thomas established in 2008. She is presently pursuing the Doctor of Psychology at California Southern University.

Faith holds an M.A. in Counselling Psychology (Hons.) from the Caribbean Graduate School of Theology and a B.Sc. in Sociology (Hons.) from the University of the West Indies (U.W.I.).

Faith has been an adjunct lecturer in the Social and Behavioural Sciences Department at the Jamaica Theological Seminary for over twenty (20) years, and at the Mico for the past ten (10) years. She has also lectured at the International University of the Caribbean (IUC), and Shortwood Teachers' College.

Faith and her husband, Donovan, are co-authors of a children's book titled *H is for Happiness,* and executive co-editor and contributing author for the book *Geared to Live: Twelve Keys to Happiness.*

Her Testimony

Faith is the first of three children for Lascelles McFarlane (deceased) and Cyriline McFarlane. Her family grew up in Harbour View, and when she was 17 years old her family moved to Bushy Park, where her mother retired from her administrative job and became a farmer, and later a contract poultry farmer with Jamaica Broilers. Her father was an accountant. From very young, Faith always wanted to be a psychologist and a missionary, and she has achieved both her dreams.

She grew up in church and got saved and baptized at Seaview Chapel Church of God in Harbour View at the age of 11 years. She started teaching Sunday School at the age of 14 years old to the 4 and 5-year-olds. When she moved to Bushy Park, St Catherine at 17 years old, there was no one teaching the 14+ age group at her new church, Spring Village Gospel Assembly, and she decided to take on the challenge of teaching them. It was a group of about 15 teens and out of this group, five (5) persons have become church leaders both locally and overseas, inclusive of two who became pastors. Faith also served as the pianist and choir director.

On leaving university, Faith answered the call to be a local missionary in the Mission Macedonia programme at Annotto Bay Baptist Church, under the leadership of Rev. Donald Lawrence, where she was the church organist and choir director. She also taught Sunday School and preached occasionally. During this time, she had a job at Marymount High School, where she taught History and was the Inter School's Christian Fellowship (ISCF) Sponsor.

She was also very active in Annotto Bay Youth For Christ, where she met and married Donovan Thomas. She served as the music director and trained the group of young people from the Annotto Bay and Buff Bay region, including the outstanding male quartet, the Schroeter Brothers. These young men went on to take the Jamaica Youth For Christ Talents for Christ stage by storm and won a trip to Grand Cayman where Faith was their chaperone.

After completing her Masters in Counselling Psychology, Faith worked at Stony Hill HEART Academy as the Senior Counsellor for 19 years. She saw her job there as a missionary in ministering to the trainees as a counsellor, in devotions and through being house leader. She trained the Stony Hill Choir for about eight years and did a number of gospel concerts in which students got saved. She also started a chapter of Youth For Christ at the Academy.

Today, Faith fellowships at Swallowfield Chapel where she has served as Sunday School Teacher, Adult Christian Education Teacher, preacher, intercessor and altar worker. Her special ministry and passion is to help hurting women and in general to help people to fulfill their life's purpose. To this end, she and her husband created a stimulating and life-changing 18-hour tertiary-level course, *The Art and Science of Happiness*. They are the main facilitators of this course.

A spin off of this course is an abridged 3-hour seminar, which has been increasingly attracting the wider educational sector, church community and business sector. The couple had the pleasure of presenting this seminar at the Jamaica Employers Federation Conference in 2018, and also in Antigua in partnership with the Halo Foundation, as guests of the Governor General.

Faith has had the privilege of being a short-term missionary in Tanzania, Swaziland, South Africa, Machilipatnam in India, Cuba and other Caribbean islands where she has spoken in seminars and pastors' training conferences.

Since April 2020, Faith and her husband have been hosting two webinars weekly, "A Covid gimme," where they invite guest speakers to present on various topics to help people live physically, emotionally and spiritually. Faith has also presented in these webinars. She and her husband also host the TV Show, GEARED TO LIVE on Mercy and Truth TV (MTM TV).

GRADUATE Q and A

Q. What are your current responsibilities professsionally and ministry wise?

A. I am the Vice President and Director of Counselling at Choose Life International. I am an adjunct lecturer at the Mico University College. I do individual, couple and group counselling. I am a motivational speaker and seminar presenter.

Q. What would you say has been your greatest contribution to society and or the kingdom of God over the years? [Don't be shy]

A. (i) I believe my greatest contribution to society and the kingdom of God has been helping people get past their past and forgive. I have several testimonies in this area and will share two that I have permission to share. The most compelling was a young lady I worked with who was in satanism (at first, without my knowledge) who initially came for counselling. She was suicidal and had some deep-seated issues that required counselling and spiritual intervention. She eventually gave her life to the Lord and through external help, was fully delivered. I worked with her until she fully forgave family members and others who had abused her. Today, over 20 years later, she is a minister in her church and a mighty woman of God.

ii.   Another outstanding case involved a young lady who had a history of abandonment and multiple abuse who was very suicidal. I worked with her on and off over a period of 8 years until she finally forgave her father for abusing her, and her mother for abandoning her. Her mother who was ill for a while eventually died. She told her mom before her death she had forgiven her, as she compassionately took care of her in the last week of her life.

iii. I was the first female preacher at Swallowfield Chapel, which started as a presentation to the women and my first message was titled, *From Misery to Ministry* in which I took the ladies on a journey of healing through forgiveness. It was an unforgettable experience. God also used me to preach to the whole congregation on Forgiveness and that too was an unforgettable experience in terms of how God ministered and showed up.

Years later, people still tell me of the impact of this ministry. I believe the Holy Spirit has anointed me to heal the broken-hearted, bind up those who are bruised, set captives free and give beauty for ashes, and the oil of joy for mourning as described in Isaiah

61, and I want to be faithful to that anointing that I believe God has placed on my life.

Q. Have you received any professional, ministry, national or regional awards? If so, name them.

A. No, not yet.

Q. Why did you attend CGST?

A. I always wanted to study psychology. I applied to go overseas after leaving 6th Form as psychology was not yet offered in Jamaica as a degree. I was accepted into a college overseas, however, God did not open the door for the financing. I went to the University of the West Indies (UWI) instead and did a BSc. in Sociology.

A few years later, I still wanted to go overseas to study psychology when my husband, who was attending Jamaica Theological Seminary at the time, told me about CGST as a new school, which was the first to be offering an M.A. Psychology in Jamaica. I checked it out, felt good about the offering and applied. I was overjoyed.

Q. What were your greatest challenges as a student and how did you overcome them? [Name 1-3]

A. *Finances.* I got two half scholarships, one of which was from CGST. I lived in Annotto Bay, St Mary, so I was away from my husband during the week as school ended at 9p.m. Mondays to Fridays. I kept my eye on the goal and did no schoolwork when I went home on weekends, as that time was dedicated to my husband. Nevertheless, it was hard on our marriage as we had only been married a year when I started CGST, but God helped us to make it work. Praise God.

Q. How has CGST impacted your life, ministry or career?

A. CGST made me very marketable. I got a job within days of graduating from CGST, as Senior Counsellor at Stony Hill Human Employment and Resource Training (HEART) Academy.

I learnt how to integrate psychology and theology and that meant a great deal to me and helped me integrate these in ministry.

On leaving my job as a Senior Counsellor, my husband and I started Choose Life International, which has as its flagship, suicide prevention. My training in psychology provided a foundation for my work in this area.

I have spoken in conferences both locally and overseas as far as Tanzania, South Africa and Swaziland in Africa, Caribbean countries, USA and India where I have spoken on topics such as Marriage, Parenting, Getting Past Your Past and others that incorporate psychological and biblical principles.

I developed the curriculum which we have been teaching at the Mico University College for the past 10 years on happiness, which is based on Positive Psychology and an integration of biblical principles. This has been utilized in a shortened form in corporate organizations, churches and schools.

Q. How has the life of Zenas Gerig impacted you?

A. He was a very compassionate man, who along with Dr. Noelliste, paved the way for me to get a financial scholarship which covered some of my cost to attend CGST.

Q. What would be your number one advice to prospective students?

A. Pray and seek God's direction for your future. If God has called you to pursue studies at CGST, he will provide the financing and whatever is needed to do so. CGST is an excellent choice for graduate school.

Q. Why would you encourage them to study at CGST?

A. CGST provides sound biblical teaching and appropriate integration of the Word with psychology in the counselling programme. Some persons pursue further studies at other colleges, and there is such a clash with their faith that they stumble and fall. CGST undergirds one's faith and encourages one to live a godly, Christ-centred life.

The graduates in the counselling programme are exemplary as they are well taught. I have had the privilege of supervising practicum students from CGST over the years and I have been very impressed with the continued high standards of professionalism and utilization of empirically based techniques and practices. CGST is a great institution for the pursuit of graduate studies, especially in Counselling Psychology. I am a proud graduate.

CGST FLAME CARRIER
Dr. Errol Joseph

Graduation: 1995, M.A. in Christian Education (Hons.)
Career: Pastor, Author and Educational Administrator/Consultant [Accreditation Coordinator, CETA]
Birthplace: Trinidad and Tobago
Married: Lorrien Joseph
Children: One, Lorrence Elton Angelo

D
r. **Errol Elton Joseph** has been the Academic Dean and President of the Open Bible Institute of Theology (OBIT) from 1976-1991, Principal of the Open Bible High School from 1991-2008 and Director of Education/Vice President, Academic Affairs at the West Indies School of Theology (WIST) from 2008-2017. He continues to lecture at WIST and at OBIT.

Dr. Joseph is the holder of a Doctor of Philosophy in Organizational Leadership, earned from Regent University. He holds a Master of Arts in Christian Education (Hons.) from Caribbean Graduate School of Theology, Bachelor of Theology (Hons) from the Jamaica Theological Seminary and Diploma in Pastoral Studies (Hons) from OBIT.

His Testimony

Dr. Joseph has been a born-again believer for over 45 years. He has extensive administrative experience in educational and church-related organizations with more than 30 years' experience with teaching in an adult education setting and approximately 29 years of combined experience in managing a theological education institute and a private high school. He was Director of Education/Vice President, Academic Affairs at the West Indies School of Theology, Maracas Valley, Trinidad & Tobago from 2008-2017. He has also served in various capacities within the Open Bible organization including Lecturer, President and Academic Dean of the Institute of Theology; Principal of Open Bible High School, President of the Trinidad and Tobago Association of Private Secondary Schools, Regional Superintendent over

20 churches and Senior Pastor of three churches over the last 27 plus years.

He is currently the pastor of the Marabella Open Bible Church. He led the curriculum development process at two institutions and participated in the successful Registration and/or Accreditation of those institutions. He also serves as Accrediting Coordinator of the Caribbean Evangelical Theological Association. He sat on several institutional boards and committees and is currently the Elder/Director of Christian Education of the Open Bible Standard Churches of Trinidad and Tobago in which capacity he chairs four (4) educational Boards and committees. In 1917 he became an associate with the Global Associates for Transformational Education (GATE) through which he participated in conducting workshops on transformational teaching and learning for theological educators throughout the Caribbean.

He has lectured in the areas of Leadership, Spiritual Formation and Conflict Management, Theology, Church History, Counselling, Current Social Issues, Research, etc. at several higher education institutions, at diploma, bachelor's and master's levels, since 1982. These institutions include the OBIT, WIST, the Caribbean Nazarene College and the Caribbean Graduate School of Theology. Dr. Joseph has extensive experience in managing conflict at both informal and formal settings at individual, church and organization levels both nationally and regionally. Since 2011, he been designing and teaching workshops, seminars and courses at church in Conflict Management and at the bachelor and master levels.

Dr. Joseph has seven publications on topics regarding theological education and leadership in education. His master's thesis was entitled "An Assessment of the Needs of the constituency of the Open Bible Institute of Trinidad and Tobago: Implications for Curriculum." His doctoral dissertation was "An Exploration of the Relationship Between Servant Leadership Attributes and Leaders' Negotiation Strategy."

Since the early 1990s, Dr. Joseph has been involved with accreditation activities serving on external evaluation teams as Secretary/Treasurer and as Accrediting coordinator of Caribbean Evangelical Theological Association for over twenty (20) years. He has attended numerous Caribbean and international conferences and has undergone extensive training as an evaluator and administrator of accreditation. He possesses considerable practical experience in the field and has conducted training in various aspects of accreditation in Trinidad and Tobago, Jamaica, Barbados, Puerto Rico and Cuba. In addition to serving as team chair and/or evaluator for visits to numerous (over 25) institutions, he is recognized as one of the elite core of evaluators and team chairs, and served as a member of the Accreditation Review Committee of the Accreditation Council of Trinidad and Tobago.

In early 2012, Dr. Joseph was engaged in a consultative role with Agencia Cubana de Estudios Teológicos (Cuban Agency for Theological Education, ACET) which was established to provide quality assurance to theological colleges in Cuba who are not covered by the government's quality assurance system. This involvement included training and the provision of guidance in the development and confirmation of accreditation standards and procedures. This led to the first external evaluation exercise of its kind being conducted in Cuba in October 2014 resulting in the accreditation of the first university outside of the government system—the Universidad Teológica Pentecostal de Cuba (Pentecostal University of Cuba) in Havana. He is also one of four (4) consultants in Quality Assurance in Higher Education from Trinidad registered with the Asia Pacific Quality Network (APQN).

GRADUATE Q & A

Q. What are your current responsibilities professionally and ministry wise?

A. Pastor of the Marabella Open Bible Church in San Fernando, Trinidad. National Elder/Director of Christian Education of the Open Bible Standard Churches Inc. in this position I am responsible for all the major organizational institutions of education and serve as the Chair of each of the Boards of the Open Bible High School (OBHS), Open Bible Institute of Theology (OBIT), Institute of Theology by Extension (INSTE) and Open Bible Children's Ministry. I also serve as Accreditation Coordinator and Executive Member of the Caribbean Evangelical Theological Association. I Lecture at the West Indies School of Theology and the Open Bible Institute of Theology and also serve as an External Evaluator for the Accreditation Council of Trinidad and Tobago.

Q. What would you say has been your greatest contribution to society and or the kingdom of God over the years?

A. I believe my greatest contribution has been in the area of theological education and training which began in 1982. During that period of time, I have served as Academic Dean, President and lecturer at the Open Bible Institute of Theology; and Adjunct Lecturer at the Caribbean Nazarene College, The Caribbean Graduate School of Theology and the West Indies School of Theology.

I also served as Secretary Treasurer, Accrediting Coordinator and Executive Member of the Caribbean Graduate School of Theology over the period 1991 to present. I served as Principal of the Open Bible High School from (1991-2008).

I have served as Academic Dean/Vice President of Academic Affairs at the West Indies School of Theology (2008-2017); President of the Association of Private Secondary Schools; and member of several government committees including the Advisory Committee to the Minister of Education, the SEMP Committee and Vision 2020 Committee on Education.

I am also a Team Chair and Evaluator for the Accrediting Council of Trinidad and Tobago and member of its Accreditation Review Committee. I have been assisting with the development of theological accreditation services for non-government evangelical institutions in Cuba, and been involved in the training of theological educators in the

Caribbean for transformational education through the Global Associates for Transformational Education.

Q. Why did you attend CGST?

A. To access training in Christian Education to better equip me as an educational administrator.

Q. What were your greatest challenges as a student and how did you overcome them?

A. My greatest challenge was in covering the cost of my education and in managing and completing the workload.

Q. How has CGST impacted your life, ministry or career?

A. Not only did CGST equip me for my role as a theological education administrator, it opened doors of additional ministry and for further training that have enhanced my personal development and my capacity to contribute to church and community

Q. How has the life of Zenas Gerig impacted you?

A. I had the opportunity to relate to Dr. Gerig more closely as a member of his spiritual support group. I was struck by his calm, consistent and committed spirit and attitude as well as by his vision and innovativeness, particularly with the development of CGST.

Q. What would be your number one advice to prospective students?

A. Maintain your relationship with the Lord and work consistently from the beginning.

Q. Why would you encourage them to study at CGST?

A. CGST is a solid evangelical institution that fosters academic excellence and adequately prepares individuals for ministry and service in the areas in which it offers training. It also provides a solid foundation for further training.

CGST FLAME CARRIER
Dr. Anthony Oliver

Graduation: 1991, M.A. in Biblical Studies
Career: Pastor and Educator (Theological Education)
Birthplace: Maracas, Trinidad and Tobago
Married: Marverlin Oliver (nee Sewell) since 1985
Children: Two (Anthony Martin Luther and Daniel Jonathan Edwards)

Rev. Dr. Anthony Oliver once served as Acting President and Academic Dean of CGST, 2006-2008. He was born in Maracas Valley in Trinidad, West Indies. He earned a PhD. from one of the leading theological institutions in the world, Trinity International University. He has been Academic Dean of three leading theological institutions in the Caribbean and Principal of Jamaica Bible College. He has pastored five (5) churches in the Caribbean over a 35-year time span while providing leadership in theological education.

His Testimony

I trusted Christ as Saviour at the age of sixteen (16). This was the most significant decision in my life. This occurred at the Woodbrook Pentecostal Church in Trinidad. I felt the need to engage in communicating the gospel of Jesus Christ and Rev. Turnel Nelson encouraged me to attend the West Indies School of Theology (WIST).

After WIST, I went on to Jamaica Theological Seminary. The Carenage Pentecostal Church granted me a full scholarship to complete the undergraduate degree; this included tuition, boarding and airfare. Thanks to Rev. Michael Brathwaite and the local church. By God's grace and provision, I moved from two "O" Levels to an earned PhD.

GRADUATE Q and A

Q. What are your current responsibilities profess-sionally and ministry wise?

A. Up until April 30, 2020, I served as Pastor, Westside Community Church, Westmoorings, Trinidad, West Indies. At present, I am Director, Transformation Today International. In addition, I am teaching at the following theological institutions in the Caribbean, namely, Caribbean Graduate School of Theology, West Indies School of Theology, and Caribbean Nazarene College. The courses I am teaching are: Old Testament Historical Books, Biblical Hebrew I, Social Change and Development and Introduction to Politics.

Q. What would you say has been your greatest contribution to society and or the kingdom of God over the years?

A. My greatest contribution to society and the kingdom of God over the years has been in the area of theological education leadership. Over a 30-year period, starting in 1987, I have been involved in providing theological education leadership as Academic Dean at Jamaica Bible College, Caribbean Graduate School of Theology, Caribbean Nazarene College and, for one year, as Acting Academic Dean at the Jamaica Theological Seminary.

I have also served as Principal, Jamaica Bible College and Acting President, the Caribbean Graduate School of Theology. In addition, I have been a part of the Theological Commission of the Caribbean Evangelical Theological Associate for over twenty years. This arm of CETA is responsible for matters pertaining to accreditation issues of regional theological institutions.

One of my major contributions to society has been my input in issues related to children at risk in Jamaica and Trinidad and Tobago. Working at the CGST in collaboration with Compassion International, I have been a part of a movement to raise awareness of various ways in which children are at risk around the world and in the Caribbean. We have also been able to focus on the 4-14 Window demographic for missions.

While firmly in the theological education arena, I have also been a pastor for many years starting in 1984.I have served as pastor of the following local churches: Mount Prospect United Brethren Church; Carenage Pentecostal Church; Cumberland Community Church; Calvary Gospel Assembly; and Westside Community Church.

Q. Have you received any professional, ministry, national or regional awards? If so, name them.

A. As it relates to awards, I will name two of them. I was the first Langham Scholar to pursue the PhD. from the Caribbean. This scholarship permitted me to do the PhD. In Theological Studies, Old Testament at Trinity International University, Deerfield, Illinois, USA. During PhD. studies I was named among the Who's Who Among American University and College Students.

Q. Why did you attend CGST?

A. After graduating from CGST in 1991, I continued studying a full year to earn the equivalence for the Master of Divinity degree, which was a matriculation requirement at Trinity International University.

I attended CGST because Professor Samuel Murrell saw potential in me while he was Academic Dean at the West Indies School of Theology (WIST). I was a WIST student and Prof. Murrell engaged me as his Teaching Assistant during the 1981 – 1982 academic year. He encouraged me to go unto Jamaica Theological Seminary (to complete the undergraduate degree), then go to CGST which was in the planning stages at the time.

He recommended that I should then go on to do doctoral work in the USA or Canada. This is exactly what happened in my life. Upon entry at WIST my plan was to complete the three-year diploma in theology and then pastor and preach throughout the region

Q. What were your greatest challenges as a student and how did you overcome them? [Name 1-3]

A. There are three (3) issues that I can identify as challenges at CGST. First, I started CGST about eight months after getting married. Further, Maverlin and I had our first child midway through that first year. So, this was really a period of great adjustment as a husband and father. We are very grateful for my mother-in-law and father-in-law who helped us care for Martin during the first couple years.

Second, it was a challenge to earn to take care of expenses related to the post graduate programme and family matters. During the first year, I sold prints of painting to care for these expenses. I sold these in offices throughout Kingston using the minibuses to move around.

During the second year (1987–1988), I started serving at the Jamaica Bible College in Mandeville. My responsibilities were Dean of Students and Dean of Academic Affairs. These new responsibilities slowed down the completion of the thesis project.

However, I gained tremendous teaching and administrative experience in the new ministry. I was teaching courses such as Introduction to Missions, History of Missions, New Testament Greek I and II, Pastoral Theology and more.

In September 1988 I was appointed Principal of Jamaica Bible College. The day the College was scheduled to be opened was September 12, 1988. That was the day Hurricane Gilbert struck Jamaica. Jamaica Bible College did not open its doors for two weeks; indeed, there was no public electricity in Kingston for almost three months.

Q. How has CGST impacted your life, ministry or career?

A. CGST has made a tremendous impact upon my life and ministry. This was the first graduate evangelical theological institution in the English-speaking Caribbean. I was privileged to be part of the very first cohort. We had the very best national, regional and international scholars teaching in the programme.

Some of these included: Dr. Garnet Roper, Dr. Samuel Murrell, Dr. Bob Edmonds, Dr. Dieumeme Noelliste, Dr. Carlton Dennis, Prof. Cullen Storey, Dr. Walter Kaiser, Jr., Dr. Narramore, Dr. Dave Carlson, Dr. Herbert Jacobsen, Dr. Tite Tienou, Dr. Dennis Magary, and many more.

When I started the PhD. at Trinity International University in 1993, CGST was on the way to being accredited. However, its reputation was such that I was admitted to Trinity's programme and passed the post admission examination with flying colours. The post admissions examination covered four areas: New Testament Theology; Old Testament Theological; Historical Theology; and Systematic Theology.

Several students from leading institutions in North America and Europe failed one or more sections of this post admission examination. This is a tribute to the quality, depth and breadth of the CGST programme. I was able to successfully defend my dissertation at the end of three years.

Q. How has the life of Zenas Gerig impacted you?

A. The life of Dr. Zenas Gerig has greatly impacted me. His wife, Mrs. Esther Gerig taught me to type, indeed, she was the typing instructor during my time at Jamaica Theological Seminary. In March 1983, Dr. Gerig encouraged me to consider pastoring a small church in the rural hills of St. Andrew. It was in a town called Mount Prospect, six miles north of Golden Spring. I started there shortly thereafter with the United Brethren. I left the Sunday before returning to Trinidad after graduation from JTS.

Also, in June 1987 when there was a vacancy at Jamaica Bible College for a Dean of Student and Academic Dean, Dr. Zenas Gerig asked me to apply for the vacancies. From Jamaica Bible College I went on to pursue the PhD. and then returned to Jamaica in 1996.

I also had the privilege of going to Missionary Church Association churches in Manchester and Westmoreland with Dr. Zenas Gerig to promote JTS while in my first year as a JTS student. There were other students on the team who would share in various ministries.

I want to point out that before graduation from JTS in 1984, Dr. Gerig informed the students about the coming Graduate School. Sometime in early 1986, he sent me a piece of correspondence indicating that CGST was going to be launched in September of that year. He invited me to apply for admission. There was a short note in the correspondence indicating that "scholarship was available." He did not say how much. But when I shared the correspondence with my wife, she was very willing for me to attend CGST.

After we got married in Jamaica in December 1985, we returned to Trinidad where I was serving as Associate Pastor, Carenage Pentecost Church. Maverlin was happy to return to Jamaica. But it all started with the correspondence from Dr. Gerig. I was the recipient of a scholarship for the two years of the programme as he had indicated. The scholarship was two third (2/3) of the tuition at the time. This was an Overseas Council Scholarship.

A few years later, when I needed to do ten (10) more courses as part of an arrangement to get M.Div. equivalence, Overseas Council provided a scholarship to me for the full sum. Years later, I found out that Dr. Charlie Spicer and his wife, President of Overseas Council at the time, told Dr. Gerig and Dr. Dieumeme Noelliste that they would underwrite this cost to help me be prepared to enter Trinity Divinity School. I am heavily indebted to Dr. Zenas Gerig and Mrs. Esther Gerig. Indeed, I am also indebted to former President, Dr. Dieumeme Noelliste, who led the negotiation with Dr. Walter Kaiser, Dean of Trinity Evangelical Divinity School at the time.

Q. What would be your number one advice to prospective students?

A. CGST is a leader in providing quality post graduate theological and counselling education in the Caribbean and whatever sacrifice you need to make to study there will be worth it.

Q. Why would you encourage them to study at CGST?

A. It will provide you with a sound theological foundation as you study any of the disciplines the institution offers.

CGST FLAME CARRIER
Ms. Erica Campbell

Graduation: 1994, M.A. in Caribbean Ministries & Master of Divinity 1996.
Career: Educator and Administrator
Birthplace: Jamaica

M s. Erica Campbell is part of the adjunct faculty of CGST. She has been a long-standing member of staff at the Jamaica Theological Seminary for over 25 years. She oversees the Bachelor of Arts in General Studies programme and is the Head of the Department of General Education with responsibilities for courses that are not credit courses, such as the English Language Proficiency Lab and Foundation Concepts in Mathematics.

Ms. Campbell is also the chair of the Assessment Committee. She pursued two degrees at CGST: The Master of Arts in Caribbean Ministries between 1992 and 1994 and the Master of Divinity between 1994 and 1996.

Her Testimony

Born to Veronica Harvey and Bentley Campbell, I grew up in Kingston Gardens, Central Kingston. All my academic pursuits and much of my spiritual formation took place while I was residing there.

I committed my life to the Lordship of Jesus Christ when I was quite young. I cannot give an exact age, but I know that when I was about nine years old and walked forward to answer the call of commitment given by Berley Adair Sr., I did so not for salvation, but I did it to publicly demonstrate my dedication to Christ.

So conscious was I of a need to testify of God's grace and sovereignty (the latter understood in concept but not in terminology at the time) that in primary school (Alpha Primary), I felt compelled to talk about Jesus Christ. Unfortunately, my shyness prevented me from being as vocal as I should have been. I felt as if I was letting God down.

Secondary school, however, provided an opportunity for me to declare who I was and who Christ is. I joined with a small group of Christians at Convent of Mercy Academy (Alpha) who met weekly and we eventually joined with the Inter-School Christian Fellowship (ISCF) at St. George's College. Dynamic and committed young people were they all. It was a blessing. Incidentally or should I say providentially and relatedly, it was during my time at Alpha that I became a member of the Personal Evangelism Group at my church through the instrumentality of Jacqueline Nelson (now Nelson-Brown) who worked at Alpha Academy for part of the time that I was a student there.

But, where I really became a bold Christian, standing up for the faith and declaring the Lordship of Jesus Christ without equivocation was at the University of the West Indies (UWI). Those were wonderful years. I fearlessly declared my allegiance to Christ in classes and made, where applicable, biblical principles central to my contribution to discussions in tutorials etc.

I also became heavily involved in the University and Colleges Christian Fellowship (UCCF). The Fellowship not only met for fellowship but was laser-focused on missions on campus. Mission activities took many forms. There was what was called "Jesustrations." And, significantly, there was ministry through creative expressions. As part of the chorale, I participated in productions put on by the group. Missions on and off campus became my life while I was at the UWI.

And then God guided me to CGST which broadened my horizons in unimagined ways.

GRADUATE Q and A

Q. What are your current responsibilities professionally and ministry wise?

A. Professional (Ministry) Responsibilities:

- I am an administrator and lecturer at Jamaica Theological Seminary.
- I oversee the Bachelor of Arts in General Studies programme.
- I am Head of the Department of General Education and am responsible for courses that are not credit courses such as the English Language Proficiency Lab and Foundation Concepts in Mathematics.
- I am the Chair of the Assessment Committee.
- I am a member of the Academic Affairs and Curriculum Management Committees.
- I lecture in the Department of General Education (Orientation to Lifelong Learning and Service, Communication Studies I and II, Introduction to Critical Thinking, Introduction to Philosophy, Introduction to Ethical Thinking) and in the Department of Theology (Hermeneutics, Theology Today, Systematic Theology etc.).

- I teach in the online programme at JTS.
- I am an adjunct lecturer at the Caribbean Graduate School of Theology.

Ministry Responsibilities (Outside of JTS):

- I teach the Discipleship Class at my local church, Assembly Hall.
- I am involved in mentoring.
- I provide ministry training and facilitate training programmes at Assembly Hall.
- I have been involved with Assembly Hall Camps and Vacation Bible School for decades and with the ISCF Discipleship Camp and Leadership Conference every year since 1996 (unbroken even by the COVID-19 pandemic thanks to virtual Meetings), first as a 96 Counsellor and a few years later as Bible Study Leader. At first, I understudied and worked very closely with Faith Linton.
- I promote literacy in Jamaican Creole and use the Jamiekan Nyuu Testament in its oral and written form in ministry.

Q. What would you say has been your greatest contribution to society and or the kingdom of God over the years?

A. As a multi-faceted person with wide-ranging areas of interest, I have been engaged in various and varied endeavours, all of which contribute to the advancement of the Kingdom of God. Interestingly, a contribution to the Kingdom of God is a contribution to society even if the latter does not recognize it to be so. Apart from my teaching and administrative work at JTS, I have made far-reaching (global) impact through:

- My involvement with Wycliffe Bible Translators. I have made presentations of the Mission Principles promoted by the organization in Jamaica, Antigua, St. Vincent and the Grenadines and in Trinidad and Tobago.
- My contribution to journals, books, and a biographic dictionary.
- My contribution to theological discourse through apologetic forums.
- Political and social analysis on LOVE 101 Radio and Television and MTV including coverage of the 2007 general elections on LOVE 101.
- Coordination of community health fairs on behalf of Assembly Hall.
- Contribution to the translation of the Jamiekan Nyuu Testament.
- Contribution to the translation of Jesus Film from English to Jamaican Creole to facilitate the voiceover.
- Playing roles in the voiceover of the Jesus Film (Jiizas Flim).

The fact that I could make an impact beyond my own shores has meant much to me. Through many of the engagements highlighted above, I have been able to contribute to cross-cultural missions though not in the way that I had originally envisioned.

Since one of my spiritual gifts is teaching, of great significance to me are the opportunities that I have had to teach the Word of God. Most fulfilling, apart from the Discipleship Class at my church, is Bible Study at the ISCF Camp and ISCF Leadership Conference. I have such a sense that I am making a difference in the lives of people which refreshes my own spirit.

I have always had a strong social conscience. From childhood, I wanted to contribute to the development of my country. I have done so through all the areas mentioned and others not mentioned. The ones more obviously fitting that understanding are the coordination of Health Fairs and the social and political analysis.

These have proven fulfilling after the fact because (1) playing the role of coordinator has taken me outside of my comfort zone (2) I have found radio and television appearances tremendously nerve-racking. It is my love for people and my understanding of my mission as a Christian to be an advocate for the vulnerable and oppressed that has helped me to overcome the inhibitions and to just act by the grace of God.

Q. Have you received any professional, ministry, national or regional awards? If so, name them.

A. I have received no national or regional ward. However, I have been acknowledged for my service by my local church and JTS.

When I was a student at CGST, I received an award for excellence from the Joint Committee for Tertiary Education.

Q. Why did you attend CGST?

A. Zadock Daniels, Berley Adair Sr. and other elders at my local church nurtured in me a love and appreciation of the Bible. I recognized it to be God's Word and was cognizant of its salvific and transforming power. I learnt so much from the teaching of godly men and women but I yearned for more and more. That yearning caused me to enroll as a student with Emmaus Bible School. It was a "school" for laymen—anyone who wanted to study the Scriptures.

The principal Noel Ellis and teachers such as Delano Palmer got me even more excited about God and His Word. I realized, however, that I needed more than Emmaus could offer and expressed that thought to Delano Palmer who introduced me to CGST. I investigated its offerings and with my interest in the Word, issues of justice and cross-cultural missions etcetera, I became convinced that it offered what I wanted. And, it did not disappoint.

Q. What were your greatest challenges as a student and how did you overcome them? [Name 1-3]

A. Working and studying was a challenge. I taught at the Queen's School at the time that I started to attend CGST. The workload from both ends was great. It meant time management and many sleepless nights, the former not a natural strength but one that was developed through necessity. The grace of lecturers and the encouragement of my colleagues were vital. Many times, study was done a few hours before a test. I am confident that paying attention in class and ruminating over course material the day after that evening class, as well as the application of analytical skills, made the difference between failure and success.

I must also say that the challenges would have been even greater without the support of my grandmother, Lucille Smith (now deceased); my brother, Christopher Campbell; and, above all, my mother, Veronica Harvey, whose middle name must be Encourager.

Q. How has CGST impacted your life, ministry or career?

A. I have always been told that I was "bright" but I never really accepted it and I believe that stifled my growth and the extent of my contribution to the kingdom. CGST put me on a path to accept my intellectual capacity and capability. Fuller realization did not come until later but that eureka moment would likely not have come without the CGST experience.

My peers; my lecturers, especially Dr. Carlton Dennis, Dr. Dieumême Noelliste and Dr. Timothy Erdel; and an encouraging friend who got me started on the journey, Delano Palmer, were pivotal."

CGST opened the door to my becoming an academic. I started the journey to learn more about God and His Word so that I could grow spiritually and make a difference at my local church as I imparted the Word of God in the available contexts. However, a wider impact was in store. Timothy Erdel helped me to see that I could operate in my spiritual gift of teaching in an academic setting.

I realized that I could make a contribution to scholarship and help in the development of persons with wide ranging influence thus expanding my own contribution to kingdom building. In addition to interaction with the students themselves, opportunities arose to minister in the settings from which they came. One such ministry opportunity was conducting Bible Studies and other sessions at Berean International Summer Camp.

My involvement with ISCF is directly attributable to my having been a student at CGST. I chose that organization as the one at which I wanted to do my internship. It was a profound life-transforming decision. Shy and reserved as I was, I was "forced", as one of my first assignments, to do oral presentations to teachers at a Teachers Christian Fellowship (TCF) Retreat. Gene Denham pushed me to exercise my gift in a setting comprised of persons with whom I was not accustomed. That one was fairly intimate but a bigger challenge was to come with a larger group of the more intimidating students. Counselling was not new, but presentations to more than 100 persons were.

Through CGST, I became more aware of what missions entailed. It was during my stint there, through the instrumentality of Delano Palmer, that I became a part of Wycliffe Bible Translators. I also became involved in promoting missions at my local church and being instrumental in getting persons involved in missions to make presentation at Sunday School and regular church services.

Q. How has the life of Zenas Gerig impacted you?

A. I have been inspired by the vision and faith of Zenas and Esther Gerig. I do not consider myself an adventurous person and one often admires others whose strengths are one's limitations. The Gerigs' pivotal roles in the formation and development of JTS and CGST signified vision through adventure becoming reality. That movement from vision to adventure to reality was a consequence of faith and a testimony to the faithfulness of God.

The Gerigs have challenged me to move outside of my own comfort zone, to take on tasks despite initial reticence and to look to God to make my work worthwhile and worthy.

Q. What would be your number one advice to prospective students?

A. Prospective students must determine to open themselves to learning. They should not just do what is necessary to get a good grade. They must want to understand so that they can become better as persons even as they hone skills necessary to make an even greater impact than they are currently making on society. I encourage students to be willing to change, to change attitudes, behaviours and even beliefs.

To prospective students I would say that if allowed, CGST will change their lives for the better. With people who have their interest at heart as administrators and lecturers, their need for holistic development should be met. I definitely recommend CGST as a choice institution.

CGST FLAME CARRIER
Dr. Rawle Tyson

Graduation: 1995, M.A. in Caribbean Ministries
Career: Pastor and Entrepreneur
Birth: July 26, 1958
Country of Origin: Jamaica
Parents: Ruby Tyson and Leo Oliver Tyson
Second of five children
Married: Esther Simpson Tyson, December 29, 1979
Children: Three (All married)
Grandchildren: Six
Disabilities: Paraplegia, Broca's Aphasia

Dr. **Rawle Tyson** is a pastor and entrepreneur who graduated in 1995 from CGST with an M.A. in Caribbean Ministries. Prior to his studies at CGST, he pursued a degree in Marine Biology from the University of the West Indies, and after CGST, a terminal degree at Columbia Theological Seminary (Doctor of Ministry). He is truly an inspiration to many. You will learn of his powerful story of a near death experience which left him paralyzed, and how God continues to use him despite tremendous challenges. His wife Esther Tyson assisted in the submission for this feature. We are truly honoured to have him in this edition of *Untold Stories.*

His Testimony: He Still Speaks

Prepared by Esther Tyson (His wife)

Rawle Tyson speaks in 2021, but not with a voice that resonates from his body. He walks powerfully, but not with legs enabled by motion. He speaks with his broad smile beaming from a body whose spine was shattered by a gunshot on December 23, 1997, with a brain that was damaged by a severe stroke that left him unable to communicate through speech or writing; yet he speaks.

Using his wheelchair as his legs since being left for dead, after being shot by gunmen on his fish farm in 1997, he reclaimed his life as a pastor, teacher of the word, counsellor, marriage officer and also as the managing director of the fish farm that he co-owned, where he was attacked.

Nothing deterred his determination to overcome in his situation and continue to bring glory to God as long as

God gave him life. He left a wheelchair on the farm that he would use to wheel around the pond banks to supervise the activities of the workers who were engaged in the day-to-day work in the ponds. He directed management meetings and organized the marketing of the products.

He was unwavering in his commitment to equip himself for more productive ministry, so that in his wheelchair. he pursued a Doctor of Ministry degree and even participated in the summer intensive course of the programme at Columbia Theological Seminary in Atlanta with his son Jonathan by his side to assist him. He graduated in April 2004, and a few weeks later suffered a massive stroke that resulted in Broca's Aphasia that severely affected his communication skills.

Yet this man, whom many love because of how much he discipled and cared for them as a young man coming up, still look to him for counsel and care. At Christian Life Fellowship, where he is one of the pastors, many persons see him on Sunday mornings in his chair smiling and being the self-appointed videographer of the service and they say to themselves, "What I am going through, I can overcome with the help of the Lord, because Pastor Rawle has been through so much but is always so pleasant and thankful." He speaks from that chair. He speaks with his smile.

He continues to speak through the messages he preached in the past. They were recorded on cassettes, as was the norm in those days, but now his mission is to convert those tapes into mp3/mp4 to post on his YouTube Channel-Dr. Rawle Tyson and on Facebook. He ministers still through these means. He affects lives by reaching out to those that he misses in church or whom the Holy Spirit lays on his heart. He still speaks.

His life gives meaning to 2 Corinthians 4:17, NIV, "For our light and momentary troubles are achieving for us an eternal glory that far outweighs them all. So we fix our eyes not on what is seen, but on what is unseen. For what is seen is temporary, but what is unseen is eternal."

As an entrepreneur, Dr. Tyson has served in various capacities including:

- A Regional Extension Officer at the Ministry of Agriculture and Fisheries (1980-1983).
- Technical Operations Manager and Production Manager at Aqua Jamaica Limited (subsidiary of Jamaica Broilers Ltd.).
- Managing Partner (with Albert Karram), at Fellowship Aqua Farm (1988-89). This partnership involved developing and managing a 30-acre pond fish farm in St. Catherine and,
- Managing Director of Fellowship Aquaculture Limited (1989-2021), operating a 48-acre fish farm facility with full integration, from brood production to marketing.

In terms of professional associations, he is a member of the World Aquaculture Society, Chairman of *Kingdom Alliance Network*, an association of churches and a Board Member of Fellowship Aquaculture Ltd.

GRADUATE Q and A

Q. What are your current responsibilities professsionally and ministry wise?

A. I am currently a co-pastor of Christian Life Fellowship. I was one of the foundation leaders of the church that was started in 1981. Due to the impact of a stroke that I suffered, my communication skills have been affected by Broca's Aphasia. I no longer do any public speaking.

I am a part of a plurality of elders that govern the church. An important role that I play among the elders is to ensure that we are maintaining a strong biblical basis on doctrines, beliefs and practices.

In addition, I participate in all meetings and decision-making processes of the leadership.

Individually, I chair the church's Community Outreach Programme. This programme covers the development of seven areas, namely; Education, Career, Entrepreneurship, Family Life Transformation, Health and Wellness and Campus Relations.

Our church is located on Gordon Town Road in Papine, St. Andrew. Our location is surrounded by informal communities with persons who need assistance in the first six areas outlined. The seventh area, Campus Relations, is of importance to our church because we straddle two of the island's major universities: The University of Technology and the University of the West Indies, Mona.

The Campus Relations programme seeks to engage these tertiary students in activities geared to leading them to Jesus Christ, strengthening the faith of those who are believers and giving them a fellowship away from home.

Q. What would you say has been your greatest contribution to society and or the kingdom of God over the years? [Don't be shy]

A. I believe that my greatest contribution to society and the kingdom of God over the years was my involvement and leadership in the revival that occurred among the youth in Jamaica in the 1970-90 period.

I got saved around 1972 while I was in 4th Form at Jamaica College. I got saved after reading the book of Revelation one Saturday. The Holy Spirit convicted me through the reading of Revelation. After I became a Christian, I went to ISCF. A revival had started in ISCF. I received the baptism of the Holy Spirit at the Dayton Avenue Church. The following year, while I was in 5th Form, a prophetic word came that Bob Bowen and I should be the presidents of ISCF. There were many prophetic words that were given at ISCF and also intense prayer and worship sessions that would last sometimes for as long as five hours.

We were involved in widespread witnessing and preaching on the bus. We went to minister at other high schools such as Hampton School, Calabar High School, Excelsior High and Meadowbrook High. The revival spread through these and many other high schools. I also became a leader of a youth meeting that was held at the University Chapel Gardens. There were many young people who were hungry and seeking after more of God. At the same time, a number of us young men from the Jamaica College ISCF became involved in Deeper Life Ministries (DLM) that led the charismatic movement at that time. We became 'shepherds' of covenant groups under DLM. Here we continued to teach and minister to other young people and even older people who wanted more of God.

We graduated from Jamaica College and started at the University of the West Indies, Mona, in 1976. I became involved with Intervarsity Christian Fellowship (IVCF). The next year, I became the Missions Secretary on the IVCF Executive Committee. This was the year in which the campus wide Missions Outreach was held. This outreach was held every four years. The culture on the campus at that time was largely influenced by the Union of Democratic Students that was communist in its ideology and ran the Students' Guild.

The Missions Committee was well-organized and spent many hours in prayer. The result was that revival swept the UWI Mona Campus in 1977. An example of the impact that this revival had on the campus was that the newly formed day IVCF meetings that would have students who lived off campus grew from 30 attendees to 300. The following year, I became president of IVCF. We decided to present a full slate of candidates from IVCF to run in the

Students' Guild elections. Our candidates swept the elections and the ethos on campus changed from communist to Christian. Emile Gabbidon, who had previously been the president of IVCF was elected as the Guild President.

During my time as president, we organized IVCF into a cell group structure; developed a discipleship programme for young men; and Sam McCook who was president of CAST IVCF and I, initiated the move to link all the IVCFs in tertiary institutions together to become University College Christian Fellowship (UCCF). Sam became the president, and I was the vice-president.

Students from all over the Caribbean were touched by this revival at the UWI. They returned home to spread the gospel of Jesus Christ. I later became a founding leader of what is now Christian Life Fellowship (CLF). This church was birthed out of a desire for persons who had been involved in the revival to have a different type of church life that more closely patterned New Testament Church life than what we were seeing at that time. A call was sent out by Christopher Duval (formerly of Jamaica College) for those of us who were leading various small groups or covenant groups to come together to birth such a church.

The church began to meet in 1981. I was one of the main teachers in the church. We believed in plurality of leadership and I was a part of the plural eldership group.

Q. Have you received any professional, ministry, national or regional awards? If so, name them.

A. No, I did not receive any awards. My ministry was cut short with my stroke in 2004.

Q. Why did you attend CGST?

A. I attended CGST to be trained in the areas that would enable me to be more prepared to serve in my pastoral ministry.

Q. What were your greatest challenges as a student and how did you overcome them? [Name 1-3]

A. One of the greatest challenges was to balance my pastoral ministry with my business responsibilities while pursuing my master's degree. The curriculum for my degree was very wide and extensive. It was therefore a huge challenge to undertake the research and readings in the in-depth way that I wanted to. Another challenge was having to attend classes in the night and to be attentive even after a full day of work.

Q. How has CGST impacted your life, ministry or career?

A. The training I received from CGST enabled me to be more impactful in my pastoral ministry of teaching the Word, counselling and church leadership.

Q. How has the life of Zenas Gerig impacted you?

A. Unfortunately, I was not acquainted with Zenas Gerig, but I am grateful for the legacy that he left in the work that he established at CGST from which I have benefited, as have so many other ministers in the Caribbean.

Q. What would be your number one advice to prospective students?

A. I think it would be better if they could gain a scholarship to pursue the course full time. Doing the course part-time is extremely challenging, and there were some students who were not able to complete the course because of the unwieldy burden that it created.

Q. Why would you encourage them to study at CGST?

A. I would encourage prospective students to choose to study at CGST because I found the programme there to be superior to similar programmes offered by other theological institutions on the island.

CGST FLAME CARRIER
Dr. Viviene Kerr

Graduation: 2000, M.A. in Counselling Psychology
Career: Educator, Administrator [President CGST], Counselling Psychologist
Birthplace: Jamaica
Children: Two

Dr. Viviene Kerr was appointed to the position of President of the Caribbean Graduate School of Theology on June 1, 2020. She is the first female president of CGST. She is an experienced Educator, Counselling Psychologist, Librarian, Administrator and Life Coach within the education and faith-based community.

Her Testimony

Dr. Viviene Kerr is from humble beginnings. Her early life began in rural Westmoreland, Jamaica, but her academic achievement transported her to the parish capital, Savanna-La-Mar, where she lived with her aunt for seven years while attending the Manning's School. She later migrated to Kingston to pursue a bachelor's degree at the University of the West Indies.

She is the penultimate of approximately twenty children of her parents. She describes her father as a typical Jamaican man who had sets of children, many of whom he neglected financially. She has lived in the homes of various family members at different stages of her life.

Prior to becoming President of CGST, Dr. Kerr has served as the Campus Registrar, Lecturer and Counselling Psychologist. She advanced to the highest position of leadership in the most challenging phase in the life of the institution. She is eminently qualified and has extensive experience in Educational Leadership; having earned a Doctor of Education degree from the Florida-based Nova Southeastern University. Dr. Kerr has served in many senior management positions in various prominent tertiary institutions.

She is an expert Information Manager, Family Life and Career Development Coach, Health Communicator, Social Psychologist and Parenting and Violence Prevention Consultant. She is a strong business development professional with a passion for entrepreneurship and for helping individuals excel to their fullest potential. She is presently the Vice Chairman of the National Parent Teachers' Association, Region 6 (St. Catherine, Jamaica). She is also the Immediate Past President of the Home School Association and Parent Representative on the Board of Management of The Cedar Grove Academy. She practices as a Counselling Psychologist at The Counselling Centre located at the Caribbean Graduate School of Theology in Kingston, Jamaica.

Prior to serving in those capacities, she worked in the areas of Librarianship, Behavior Change Management and Higher Education as a Lecturer and University Registrar in various government and educational institutions in Jamaica. She has occupied several senior positions within the Library and information Association of Jamaica, serving for two consecutive terms as its President between the years 2014-2016.

One of her assignments which she treasures involves her assignment as the Clarendon Parish Coordinator in the Youth.Now (Adolescent Reproductive Health Project). That experience gave her the opportunity to work directly with the education and faith-based communities. Through that assignment with the Ministry of Health, she utilized the knowledge and skills gained at CGST to educate families, counsel teens, and teach them the critical life skills that they needed to navigate the challenges they faced.

She was married, but that union ended. She has two beautiful children, Rashaw and Desiree.

GRADUATE Q and A

Q. What are your current responsibilities professsionally and ministry wise?

A. Professional responsibilities include:

- President of CGST—Administrative Leadership, Student Recruitment, Fundraising, Partnership Development and Lecturer and Counselling Psychologist.
- Counselling Psychologist—Establish partnerships for the provision of psychological services to distinct groups and the provision of psychological support to clients when available.
- Education Consultant—provides expert know ledge, advice and guidance to parents, teachers and school administrators
- Coaching services—Career guidance, Educational Financing in Higher Education and the provision of Research Supervision of Graduate and Doctoral students.
- Vice Chairman, NPAJ Region 6 — Oversees the Finance and Training portfolio, organizing and participating in seminars, workshops and

other fora for the training of PTA presidents and parents.

Ministry include:

- Executive member of the Family Life Ministries (FLM) of the New Testament Church of God, Braeton—plan, organize, and assist in implementing the FLM agenda. Speaker on family life matters.
- Member of the National Missions Department—assist with the planning and organizing of mission-related projects across Jamaica.
- Member of the Braeton NTCOG Prison Ministry—assisting with the planning, organizing and implementation of religious and welfare services such as delivery of care packages to the female inmates at the Camp Road facility (previously located in Fort Augusta in Portmore, St. Catherine).
- Member of the Children's Home Ministry—assisting with the planning, organizing and implementation of visits and the provision of care packages and counselling services to the residents of the Yadel Home for Girls located in St. Catherine.

Q. What would you say has been your greatest contribution to society and or the kingdom of God over the years?

A. My greatest contribution to society has been the management of information systems required to enable the provision of information needed to solve problems, advance the educational process, and improve people's lives. I am an educator who is concerned with empowering people to fulfill their purpose.

I have also contributed significantly to the field of Counselling Psychology, serving my denomination and the educational system in Jamaica. As an educator with a passion for teaching adults, I have taught many persons both within various higher educational institutions and within the workplace how to integrate the knowledge they have gained educationally with the requirements of the world of work.

Q. Have you received any professional, ministry, national or regional awards? If so, name them.

A. Awards and Honours:
- Vice-Chairman, National Parent Teachers Association, Region 6
- HSA Representative on The Cedar Grove Academy Board of Management 2019/2020 and 2020/2021
- HSA President, 2018/2019
- LIAJA Award for Community Service, 2016
- LIAJA President, 2014/2015 and 2015/2016
- Several workplace awards such as Exceptional Planner and acknowledgement for the organization of specific educational opportunities for the library profession while

at the Planning Institute of Jamaica, 2012 and 2014

Q. Why did you attend CGST?

A. I was dissatisfied with the unavailability of professional counsellors within the church community, and I wanted to be equipped to serve Christians who needed counselling.

Q. What were your greatest challenges as a student and how did you overcome them? [Name 1-3]

A. 1) Balancing family, school and work commitments —I sought assistance from my family and employer (utilized my vacation leave to do practicum).

2) Managing the disintegration of my marriage while providing counselling support to persons - I sought counselling at school and privately.

3) Managing a chronic illness and completing my programme within the anticipated timeline—I took a year off to allow my health to improve.

Q. How has CGST impacted your life, ministry or career?
A. CGST has had a profound impact on my life, ministry and career. My present job of being the president of CGST is testament to that effect. CGST has equipped me to integrate psychology with my faith in

God. I am able to seamlessly present on any topic while integrating my belief without causing offence. My life is now one of sacrifice where I yield to God's will and direction without putting up resistance. I have grown spiritually, intellectually and financially. I am a more effective minister of the Gospel of Jesus Christ. My present assignment has altered or delayed my plan to migrate.

In 2019, I was finally moving in the direction of becoming the full-time Psychologist and Life Coach I dreamt of becoming when I was offered the job as the Campus Registrar. Figuring that I would have completed my relocation plans within the contractual year, I decided to accept the part-time engagement. I continued the part-time coaching and professional counselling services I started. Little did I know that the Lord had other plans for me.

Q. How has the life of Zenas Gerig impacted you?

A. The life of Dr. Zenas Gerig has impacted me and CGST tremendously. My being a Jamaican-born and bred president is an example of his dream for the administration of theological education within the Caribbean. It was his work that resulted in the establishment of this institution and through his son, now the Acting chairman of CGST (2020), and his family, the institution has continued to benefit significantly from Dr. Gerig's legacy. The family's most recent contribution has been in the development of our IT infrastructure and they continue to support the present administration morally and financially.

Q. What would be your number one advice to prospective students?

A. If you want to do graduate work in Theology or Psychology and you are a Christian, CGST should be your first choice.

Q. Why would you encourage them to study at CGST?

A. I would inform them that there are at least three factors that make the graduate school a preferred choice for Christians:

- The quality of its programmes, lecturers, and its reputation has been the formidable ingredients for CGST success over the years.

- The ability to focus on its core programmes, which are a Master of Arts in Counselling Psychology and a Master of Arts in Theology.

- Its role as a Christian institution in enhancing the growth and development of Jamaica and the Caribbean region.

CGST is now offering more short-term courses, to cater to individuals who might not necessarily want to study for a long period of time. Other programmes currently being worked on include a continuous education scheme for graduates from the Counselling Psychology programme and courses to help pastors and other church members navigate the online space.

As an institution, we have the best counselling psychology programme in Jamaica, and, possibly, the Caribbean. Our graduates have excelled in their fields of study. Many are known public figures who have contributed and are contributing to national and regional development.

At CGST, we focus on equipping our students to be strategic in reaching those who are hurting. We offer programmes steeped with professional rigour and a strong biblical foundation. Based on our experience, we recognize that there is no good health without mental health and a healthy population is needed to ensure that Jamaica achieves developed country status by 2030. When our people are mentally and spiritually healthy, they are more productive. This will lead to economic growth and prosperity and fewer reports of corruption.

CGST has also ensured that all our current and prospective students have access to all our programmes online. We are expanding our reach in the Caribbean by partnering with our Caribbean, and other overseas-based institutions to forge and build alliances that will be beneficial to our students and the school.

Finally, I would inform them that our programmes are designed with cultural context in view. This exposure ensures relevance and enables our graduates to be better equipped to serve in the region. CGST offers quality adult education and is accredited both locally and regionally and we continue to improve on systems already in place to ensure and maintain high academic standards.

CGST FLAME CARRIER
Dr. Joan Pinkney

Graduation: 2001, M.A. Counselling Psychology
Career: Educator, Counselling Psychologist and
Administrator (Manager, The Jamaican Copyright
Licensing Agency)
Birthplace: Jamaica
Married: Vincent Pinkney
Children: Three

Dr. Joan Pinkney holds a Doctor of Philosophy in Family Studies from Oxford Graduate School, Tennessee, and an honorary doctor of Science in Psychology from the CGST. She is a graduate of Jamaica Theological Seminary and CGST where she earned a Bachelor of Arts in General studies with emphasis in Guidance and Counselling and a Master of Arts in Counselling Psychology respectively.

Dr. Pinkney has been an adjunct lecturer in Psychology, Business Ethics, Conflict Management and Counselling at several tertiary institutions in Jamaica. She is a licensed practicing Counsellor and holds the position of Manager—Licensing and Member Services at The Jamaican Copyright Licensing Agency.

Her Testimony

Joan Pinkney is the sixth child for her parents Kenneth and Alzie Russell. Her father Kenneth was a lay-preacher and managed a Church in a District called Nutfield, in St. Mary, Jamaica. She remembers that each time he preached, she went to the altar. She was baptized in 1971 at age 14. Joan has been walking with the Lord ever since. She attributes her teaching, leadership, counselling and preaching skills and inspiration to her parents who not only performed those roles but were very impactful in the communities they served.

Joan's skills as a motivational speaker, Counselling Psychologist, lecturer and workshop/seminar facilitator are in high demand. She has facilitated workshops, seminars and conferences locally and overseas, as well as counselling/psychotherapy with corporate entities, tertiary institutions, secondary and primary schools, church groups and other social groups in matters related but not limited to: human resource management, sexuality, parenting training, marriage enrichment, retirement, mate selection, managing adolescence, suicide, stress and grief management, career guidance and midlife crises.

It should be noted that with a background in General Insurance, Human Resource Management and Administration, Joan has a sound understanding of the general dynamics within an office setting. This places her at an advantage in integrating her Counselling skills in order to address and recommend interventions for general and specific situations of concern.

Joan is a writer, an actress and a noted resource person on several local radio and television stations in Jamaica on matters of social concerns and mental health. She also hosts the programme "The Counsellor" aired on Love 101 FM, Jamaica.

She makes time for play and enjoys aerobics, stimulating conversations and movies, and still delights in the close interaction with her three (3) adult children and one grandchild. Among the committees and agencies with which she gives voluntary service, Joan is a director of JAMPAS – The Jamaica Parent School and in 2012, she produced three motivational e-Books entitled: *Self-Esteem My Child and Me, Sexuality Head-on and Wounded.*

GRADUATE Q & A

Q. What are your current responsibilities professsionally and ministry wise?

A. Professional:

- *Manager,* Licensing & Client Services—Jamaican Copyright Licensing Agency [Sells and manages licensing portfolio, Solicits and manages Affiliates' portfolio; Other administrative duties
- *Lecturer:* Psychology, Counselling and Business Ethics
- *Counselling Psychologist:* Practicing Counsellor —Telepsychology
- *Facilitator:* Corporate/Other—Conferences, Webinars and Workshops

Ministry - Local Church:

- Young Adult Sunday School Teacher
- Member of Counselling Ministry
- Member of Nominating Committee
- Member of Singing Group
- Regularly participates in preaching assignments

Ministry – Other:

- Counselling—Radio Show host
- Facilitator—Regularly participates in Church related Conferences, Workshops and Webinars

Q. What would you say has been your greatest contribution to society and or the kingdom of God over the years?

A. These are:
  i. Lecturing: Facilitated the growth and development of individuals who in turn are making marked impact in their vocation worldwide
  ii. Counselling services: offered to listeners on Counselling Radio show—listenership extends to USA, Europe and England, Caribbean, Africa, Australia based on reports
  iii. Webinars/Conference deliveries—impactful, sound information and life-changing presentations
  iv. Preaching assignments: impactful, insightful and spirit filled delivery

  v). 3 E-books: Published in 2012 [*Wounded; Self Esteem my child and me and Sexuality Head-on*]

2b. Have you received any professional, ministry, national or regional awards? If so, name them.
  i. Jamaica Theological Seminary – Valedictorian
  ii. Caribbean Graduate School of Theology – Valedictorian

iii.   Oxford Graduate School – Chancellor's Award [at Graduation PhD]

Q. Why did you attend CGST?

A. I felt the calling of God to further enhance my training as a counsellor having graduated from JTS with a minor in Guidance and Counselling. CGST seemed a natural choice.

Q. What were your greatest challenges as a student and how did you overcome them?

A.

i.   *Facing me and the painful realities of my past and current life experiences.* Counselling was a great help. I was guided toward accepting forgiveness from God, forgiving myself and forgiving others who had hurt me. I was also guided how to deal with the abusive relationship I was living in at the time.

ii.   The Comprehensive Exam was a challenge. Studying times were rather intense.

Q. How has CGST impacted your life, ministry or career?

A. The experience at CGST afforded me training in academic, personal and spiritual areas of life. The concept of integration became more real while at CGST. I became more appreciative of the fact that as a child of God everything I do whether 'secular' or church-related are "part and parcel" of my life's ministry. All I do must always honour and glorify God.

Q. How has the life of Zenas Gerig impacted you?

A. I am grateful that Dr. Zenas Gerig was obedient to God and carried out the vision and mission which founded both JTS and CGST. His obedience has created opportunities for thousands of individuals including myself to be trained in the area of their calling toward fulfilling God's purpose. Without his obedience, I likely would not be writing this narrative today.

Q. What would be your number one advice to prospective students, and why would you encourage them to study at CGST?

A. The training experience at CGST offers not only hard skills (academics), but soft skills (e.g. empathy) which are vital to an integrative approach for effectiveness in career and ministry engagements. Most institutions that offer similar training do not include spiritual development. CGST without offering a specific course in "spiritual" development, integrates this subtly yet gracefully throughout the programme. If one needs that kind of interaction, CGST is unquestionably the place to be.

CGST FLAME CARRIER
Dr. Earlmont Williams

Graduation: 2002, M.A. in Intercultural Studies (High Honours); 2006, Master of Divinity (M.Div.) High Honours

Career: Ordained Bishop (Pastor) and School Administrator (Academic Dean)

Birthplace: St. Vincent and the Grenadines

Married: Sydonie Williams

Children: Two (Earlmont Jr. and Kharisma)

Rev. Dr. Earlmont Williams graduated twice from the CGST in 2002 and 2006. Originally from St. Vincent and the Grenadines, he now lives in Jamaica and is an Ordained Bishop in the New Testament Church of God in Jamaica. He is the Academic Dean at Bethel Bible College of the Caribbean; pastor of the Georges Valley New Testament Church of God and the District Overseer of the Georges Valley District of Churches in Manchester, Jamaica; a Marriage Officer, Bible teacher, seminar/workshop presenter, radio discussant, crusade preacher, and convention speaker. He has preached in many churches and other contexts in Jamaica, the Caribbean, and the United States of America.

His Testimony

Rev. Earlmont Marc Macaine Williams is the second of his mothers' two children. He grew up in Byera Village on the windward side of the island and in Prospect in the central part of St. Vincent and the Grenadines. He attended the Byera Anglican Primary School, the Calliaqua Anglican School, the St. Vincent Grammar School, and the St. Vincent Bible College. He got saved at a youth camp in 1993 and became a member of the Georgetown New Testament Church of God where he was elected as the youngest member of the Church and Pastor's Council and served as a Sunday school teacher within two years of becoming a Christian.

Rev. Williams came to Jamaica in 1997 to pursue a bachelor's degree in Theology at Bethel Bible College. He completed his internship at the Georges Valley New Testament Church of God, where he now serves as pastor since September 2010. He graduated from Bethel with First-Class Honours in the year 2000. After praying about whether he should pursue graduate studies or enter the pastorate, he sensed that the former was God's will for him at that time in his life. Therefore, in the year 2000 he applied to the Caribbean Graduate School of Theology to read for the Master of Arts in Interdisciplinary Studies with an emphasis in Counselling Psychology. He graduated in 2002 with High Honours.

In 2003, Rev. Williams decided to pursue a Master of Divinity (MDiv) degree at the Graduate School. However, he was moved by the Spirit of God in 2004 to enter the pastorate in the Church of God while he was still teaching at the Jamaica Theological Seminary (JTS). In February 2005, Rev. Williams assumed pastoral duties for the first time in the Church of God, specifically the Duhaney Park congregation. He shepherded this church for two years while he was the Registrar of the Jamaica Theological Seminary. In June 2006, he graduated from the CGST Master of Divinity programme with High Honours.

In March 2007, Rev. Williams was reassigned to the Rhoden Crescent church in the Olympic Gardens community as its Associate Pastor alongside Bishop John Hardy. He served at this church for one (1) year and five (5) months. He was also reassigned at the Jamaica Theological Seminary in September 2007 to the Academic Affairs Division as the Quality Assurance Coordinator and Acting Head of the Department of Behavioural and Social Sciences.

Rev. Williams resigned from JTS in August 2008 after the Administrative Bishop assigned him to serve as pastor of the Battersea church in Mandeville and as Academic

Dean of Bethel Bible College, which is also situated in Mandeville. He pastored the Battersea church for two years, from September 2008 to August 2010. The highlight of Dr. Williams' academic journey came in September 2015 when he earned the Doctor of Philosophy degree in the Integration of Religion and Society at the Oxford Graduate School (now called Omega Graduate School) in Dayton, Tennessee, USA.

Rev. Williams still serves as the Academic Dean of Bethel Bible College of the Caribbean Jamaica (as it is called now) as well as the Biblical Hebrew and Biblical Greek lecturer at that institution. He served in various capacities at the Jamaica Theological Seminary for 15 years. He has taught at both the bachelor's and master's levels at other tertiary institutions, including the International University of the Caribbean (IUC), and the Caribbean Graduate School of Theology. Finally, he has been a Quality Assurance Assessor with the Jamaica Tertiary Education Commission (J-TEC) since May 2017.

GRADUATE Q and A

Q. What are your current responsibilities professsionally and ministry wise?

A. As a pastor, I carry out the following responsibilities:

    a. Offer strategic leadership to the Church Council and entire faith community

b. Administer two major sacraments—Communion and Baptism
c. Oversee the administrative operations of the church
d. Offer passionate worship leadership
e. Lead the church's community outreach efforts
f. Engage in pastoral visitation
g. Initiate leadership training sessions
h. Oversee the evangelistic efforts of the local church
i. Supervise the departmental leaders and other volunteers
j. Engage in service planning on a quarterly basis
k. Supervise church and community development projects
l. Offer solution-focused individual, marriage and family counselling.

As District Overseer, I engage in the following:
a. Organizational administration. Do pioneering work in organizing and mobilizing the Georges Valley District of Churches.
b. Event management. Planned, organized and hosted a District Launching and Induction Service.
c. Fulfillment of all the responsibilities outlined in the Minutes of the International General Assembly of the Church of God (Cleveland).
d. Mentoring and coaching. Serve as a mentor/coach to the ministers and their families in the district.

e. Offering pastoral care and guidance. Serve as a pastor to the ministers and their families in the district.

f. Organizational monitoring and control. Monitor the progress of all the churches in the district.

g. Planning and promotional work. Promote the national programmes on the district, plan district meetings, and assist the Administrative Bishop in planning evangelistic and training ministries on the district.

As Academic Dean of BBCC-J, the following are my duties and responsibilities:

a. Oversee the strategic directions and daily operations of the Academic Department

b. Supervise all the lecturers in the programmes of the College

c. Supervise one (1) administrative assistant

d. Chair the Academic Council, the Examination Committee, and the Faculty Council

e. Implement quality assurance system based on the standards of the University Council of Jamaica.

f. Co-chair the Self-Study Committee and lead the process of preparing for UCJ re-accreditation of Bethel's programmes.

g. Implemented changes in Bethel's academic advising, examinations, instruction and grade reporting processes.

h. Prepare all the application documents as required by the UCJ for the reaffirmation of accreditation of the College's programmes.

i. Review all the College's course outlines or syllabi as a part of the UCJ's requirements for reaffirmation of accreditation.

j. Lead in the process of reviewing the College's Catalogue, Student Handbook, Strategic Plan, and Staff and Faculty Handbook.

k. Generate and enact new academic policies to enhance the College.

Q. What would you say has been your greatest contribution to society and or the kingdom of God over the years? [Don't be shy]

A. Based on my numerous experiences within the sanctuary and in the seminary, I think my greatest contribution to the kingdom of God and to society in general is the fact that I have helped significantly to shape the lives and ministry skills of younger pastors and other Christian ministers and workers who have gone on to bring about transformation in churches, schools, workplaces, and communities.

Q. Have you received any professional, ministry, national or regional awards? If so, name them.

A. No, I have not.

Q. Why did you attend CGST?

A. I attended CGST because I heard that it was an excellent graduate school that offered programmes in theology and divinity, areas of study in which I was interested at the time. A few of my lecturers were enrolled in CGST programmes while I was in college, and they spoke highly and glowingly about CGST. I decided that I would pursue graduate studies based on their testimonials regarding CGST, which they claimed was a life-transforming institution.

Q. What were your greatest challenges as a student and how did you overcome them? [Name 1-3]

A. When I entered to pursue graduate studies, I was placed on probation because the college where I completed my first degree did not yet have any accredited programmes. I found that to be a huge set-back and challenge at the outset. However, I knew that, based on my outstanding performance in that first degree programme, I would do a great job in the M.A. programme. I faced the challenge with great confidence and God's help and by the second semester of my first year, the probation was lifted.

Another challenge I faced had to do with the paucity of funds that I had at my disposal to complete the programmes, especially the M.A. in Interdisciplinary Studies. It could be said that it was a humongous challenge. However, I sought and received assistance from my father and other relatives, and I also obtained a few scholarships from CGST. Hence, I was able to complete both programmes.

Yet another challenge that I had to overcome was the Comprehensive Exams that I had to do at the time.

I saw this component of my programmes as a mountainous hurdle that I had to jump over with much effort and God's grace. I joined a study group and did additional work on my own and I was able to meet that challenge.

Q. How has CGST impacted your life, ministry or career?

A. CGST has had a transformational and destiny-shaping impact on my ministry, career path, and life in general. The rigour and general quality of the academic input and ministry formation that I experienced prepared me to serve as a pastor, lecturer, and educational administrator. If I had not attended CGST, I do not know whether I would have been able to travel along the path that I have travelled professionally and vocationally.

Q. How has the life of Zenas Gerig impacted you?

A. Zenas Gerig was a giant of a man. I met him once on my journey through CGST. He did not teach me; nor was I privileged to have served under his leadership. However, because he was the trailblazer in the establishment of both JTS and CGST, which contributed significantly to my empowerment and preparation for Christian ministry and professional engagement in the seminary, he played a secondary role in my formation. Therefore, he has impacted my life and ministry indirectly through the two mentioned institutions.

Q. What would be your number one advice to prospective students?

A. I would advise them to begin with a positive and progressive mindset and allow the institution to shape and mold them into the transformational servant leaders and professional helpers that God would like them to become.

Q. Why would you encourage them to study at CGST?

A. I would encourage them to study at CGST because it is not just another educational institution that offers graduate degrees and other programmes. This institution empowers people for service, enlarges their professional and ministry borders, endows them with the academic foundation for doctoral studies, and enriches their lives. After studying at CGST, graduates can go anywhere in the world and bring about transformation in their spheres of influence, ministry, and service.

CGST FLAME CARRIER
Rev. Courtney Anthony Stewart

Graduation: 2008, Masters in Business Administration
Career: Pastor and Administrator (General Secretary of Bible Society of the West Indies)
Birthplace: Jamaica
Married: Ingrid Stewart
Children: Four children (3 biological daughters and a foster daughter)

Rev. Courtney Stewart is an ordained Christian minister and the General Secretary of Bible Society of the West Indies. He graduated with a Master of Business Administration from CGST in 2008. He pursued undergraduate studies at the Jamaica Theological Seminary, graduating as the youngest student at that time with a Bachelor of Theology degree. He spearheaded the translation of the New Testament into the Jamaican language and the publication of "Di Jamiekan Nyuu Testiment" (The Jamaican New Testament), the largest extant corpus of work in the Jamaican language.

His Testimony

Born in the Whitfield Town area of St. Andrew, Jamaica, he is the first of two children gifted to Reginald, a policeman and Una, a dressmaker. His formative years were spent in the Whitfield Town community where he attended the Whitfield Town Primary School from which he took and passed the Common Entrance Examination, earning him a place at the Calabar High School. It was while in high school that Courtney committed his life to the Lord and sensed a call to full-time Christian service. He applied to and was accepted to read for a Bachelor of Theology (B.Th.) degree at the Jamaica Theological Seminary, graduating at 20 years of age.

Rev. Stewart was ordained to the Christian ministry in December 1981 and has served in pastorates in both rural and corporate areas. In November 1993, he joined the staff of Bible Society of the West Indies (BSWI) and has been serving as its General Secretary since then, overseeing the territories of Belize, Bahamas, Cayman Islands, Jamaica and the Turks and Caicos Islands. He has served on committees and boards of the parent body, the United Bible Societies (UBS), travelling extensively abroad attending and participating in many of its gatherings on all five continents.

A signal event under Stewart's leadership at the BSWI was the translation of the New Testament into the Jamaican language and the publication of "Di Jamiekan Nyuu Testiment" (The Jamaican New Testament). This project received much media attention and captured the interest and emotions of persons (Jamaicans and non-Jamaicans) across the world. Rev. Stewart became the face of this controversial project resulting in the BBC sending a crew to Jamaica to interview him and others concerning their views on this undertaking.

For several years, while a member at the Tarrant Baptist church in Kingston, Jamaica, Rev. Stewart served as chairman of the Board of Management of its radio ministry, **The Breath of Change, TBC Radio - 88.5 FM.** A community radio station, it started its initial on-air presentation for just three hours daily which blossomed into six hours, then 12 hours and eventually became a 24-hour radio station offering a wide range of programmes including news, weather, preaching and other features while marinating its focus on presenting the Gospel of Jesus Christ in an essentially music format.

A community person, Rev. Stewart served on the St. Richard's Primary School Board as the PTA's representative for many years while his children were students there and was asked by the PTA to continue serving in that capacity even after his children had left the school and were enrolled at university. He currently serves on the board of the Kingston Parish Library. Rev. Stewart is also an iterant preacher. He and his family are regular worshippers at Mona Baptist Church.

GRADUATE Q & A

Q. What are your current responsibilities professsionally and ministry wise?

A. I continue to serve as the General Secretary of the Bible Society of the West Indies with responsibility for the management and welfare of the organization. I am also an itinerant preacher to whom many pulpits have been opened across denominational lines and overseas, for which I am very grateful to the Lord.

Q. What would you say has been your greatest contribution to society and or the kingdom of God over the years?

A. I suspect that would be a 2-fold response.

i. It would be the introduction of the Good News Translation as the Bible of choice to be used in the primary schools instead of the King James Version, which the majority of children do not understand. This was a major undertaking over several years.

ii. Perhaps the greater contribution is the translation, publication and distribution of the New Testament in Jamaican Creole (Patwa). This was the most massive undertaking both in terms of scope, cost and promotion. The project made the news in many countries and I was interviewed by the BBC and other major news media in the UK several times over the four years of this project.

Q. Why did you attend CGST?

A. I attended CGST because I wanted formal training in management, considering that I was managing a Christian organization in an ever-changing environment. The fact that the programme was being offered by an evangelical Christian graduate school made it even more appealing as they would be sensitive and disposed to the Christian commitment of the student. The icing on the cake for me was the modular programme that was offered on the weekends, as I would not have been able to pursue the programme if it was offered on a full-time basis.

Q. What were your greatest challenges as a student and how did you overcome them?

A. There were:

i. **Self-doubt:** I wanted to pursue the programme, but it had been so long that I was in a formal institution of higher education that I wondered if I would have been able to manage the study, the exams and just be able to keep up with the programme and its requirements. The encouragement of friends, colleagues and the other students in the programme who were basically in my age cohort made me realize that I was not alone and others were also in my shoes or had walked in similar shoes before. The camaraderie among the students also made it manageable.

ii. **Travelling:** My responsibilities here at BSWI entail a fair bit of traveling. At the time of doing the programme I was traveling a great deal and as much as I would try and work around the programme, such as leaving Jamaica on the Sunday and returning as early as I could on the Friday or even on Saturday morning so that I would catch most of the all-day class, it was still a challenge. In one instance I recall being away in Brazil for almost half of the module and turning up for the exam wondering if it made any sense. I overcame this challenge via technology and with the support of the colleagues in my group. They would send me the notes via email, I would complete the assignments at night and email them to the lecturer, and I was the editor for the group assignments. The empathy and support of my group members brought me through on several occasions.

iii. **Family**: Being present with but absent from my family was also a challenge. Because of assignments, work commitments and other engagements, it was difficult being involved with and in all the aspect of family life to which I was accustomed. I forgot dates and activities and was unable to attend and participate in aspects of the girls' lives that I really regret. My wife, Ingrid, understood my challenges and had to work overtime to make up for my lack and for this I am eternally grateful. As the girls became older, they understood and appreciated what I was going through.

Q. How has CGST impacted your life, ministry or career?

A. Perhaps the greatest impact I can recall was a presentation that I had to make before my board of directors at the Bible Society. I employed a PowerPoint presentation and the treasurer who was a bank manager declared to the group that the format and contents of the presentation were what one expects from someone who has an MBA degree. It was a tremendous affirmation. It also served to inspire confidence in my capacity to understand issues, grapple with divergent positions, and arrive at considered opinions with the supporting arguments.

Q. How has the life of Zenas Gerig impacted you?

A. As a 17-year-old enrolling at JTS I was struck by the warmth and embrace of this gentleman. He was always willing to listen to me and to share his thoughts and offer advice in an atmosphere of appreciation of my circumstances. The student body was quite small, so he would sometimes have meals with us and was always ready to go out of his way to support me. I was impacted by this approach and have sought to always be available and ready to assist and support those who are in genuine need, even if it is only to lend a sympathetic and empathetic ear.

Q. What would be your number one advice to prospective students?

A. Know why you want to go to CGST and seek to give it your very best, not just for the grades but also for the knowledge you will garner and the relationships that you will form.

Q. Why would you encourage them to study at CGST?

A. I was struck by the fact that the lecturers were just as open to learning from the students as we were to learn from them. I recall disagreeing with a point expressed by a lecturer and sharing my reasons for so doing. I was struck by his response. After further discussion and explanation, he agreed with me and changed his position. I found the classroom at CGST to be a place of rich learning; from the text, from the lectures, from the interactions, and from life experiences and from the devotions.

Remembering
Dr. Yvette Veronica Stupart
and
Mrs. Patricia Eves-McKenzie

Unfortunately, both of these outstanding women passed away before the completion of this book, and did not get a chance to answer the graduate feature questions. They both had consented in writing to be part of this project, and this book would not be complete without their stories.

Even in death, both women continue to change lives. By including them, the world will hear their stories and lives will be changed across the globe. In fact, this part of the book will close with an inspirational leadership charge from Mrs. Eves McKenzie on the importance of serving and investing in the lives of others.

CGST FLAME CARRIER
Dr. Yvette Veronica Stupart

Graduation: 2000, M.A in Counselling Psychology (Hons.)
Career: Counselling Psychologist, Educator, Administrator [Head of the Department of Behavioural and Social Sciences, CGST]
Birthplace: Jamaica
Married: Dr. Copeland Stupart
Children: One (Jason)
Death: December 18, 2020

D r. Yvette Veronica Stupart described herself in her LinkedIn profile as "a purpose-oriented person. I strive to make a difference in the lives of others as I embrace God's purpose for my life." She served as a Justice of the Peace for the Parish of St. Catherine and received her PhD in Counsellor Education and Supervision from Regent University in 2010. Her dissertation title was, "An Exploration of Counsellor Supervision in Jamaica."

We have preserved Dr. Stupart's testimony here using portions of her eulogy and profile on LinkedIn. She graduated with honours from CGST in 2000 with an M.A. in Counselling Psychology. She had an unmistakable devotion to CGST. Later in 2014, she became the Head of the Department of Behavioural and Social Sciences at CCGST and remained as such until her passing in December 2020. Her responsibilities included:

- Coordinating the Counselling Psychology Pro-gramme
- Managing and supervising the staff in the Coun-selling Centre
- Providing academic advisement to students in the relevant aspects of the programmes
- Providing supervision of practicum administrator and supervisors
- Participating in meetings of the Academic Affairs Committee
- Preparing and presenting development plans for the department

- Assisting with the periodic internal self-study of the Graduate School for accreditation
- Fostering and encouraging research productivity among teaching staff for publishing, leadership development, and development of professional practice.

Her testimony and other notable achievements have been captured in her eulogy, submitted by her husband, Dr. Copeland Stupart.

Remembering Dr. Yvette Veronica Stupart

Our hearts can sing when we pause to remember;
A heartache here is but a stepping stone,
Along a trail that's winding always upward;
This troubled world is not our final home.

The words of Proverbs 31 capture the essence of Dr. Yvette Stupart. Who can find a virtuous woman for her price is far above rubies? The heart of her husband doth safely trust her, so that he shall have no need of spoil. She will do him good and not evil all the days of her life. She seeketh wool, and flax and worketh willingly with her hands. She is like the merchants' ships, she bringeth her food from afar. She riseth also while it is yet night, and giveth meat to her household, and a portion to her maidens. Her children arise up and call her blessed; her husband also, and he praiseth her.

Dr. Stupart began her earthly journey in Nine Turns, Clarendon on 30th of July 1955. At the tender age of six, she was enrolled at the Toll Gate All Age School in Clarendon, where she spent a short time. She moved on to Baileston Primary then re-entered Toll Gate in time to sit the Common Entrance Examination, which saw her transitioning to Vere Technical High School. Upon graduating from Vere, she worked for a short time as a pre-trained teacher at May Pen Secondary, now Central High School. She was later accepted at Mico Teachers' College now Mico University College where she successfully completed a course of studies in Secondary School Education in the Sciences, which made her a well accomplished trained teacher.

She was first employed at St. Hugh's High School as a Science teacher where she gained further experience in building her skills as an educator. She later enrolled at the University of the West Indies (UWI) to pursue a Bachelor of Science Degree in Public Administration. While there, she met the love of her life Copeland, who later became her husband. Upon completing her studies at UWI in 1987, she worked for a short time at the Jamaica Telephone Company as a Job Analyst. In 1988, she gained employment at St. Annie's Secondary School as an Integrated Science teacher.

Yvette served with class and dignity as she was determined to leave a mark on the minds of those entrusted to her supervision. After leaving St. Annie's Secondary School she gained employment at Waterford High School as an Integrated Science teacher. While at Waterford High School she moved up the ranks to the Head of the Science Department, and Vice Principal. During her time at Waterford High School, she travelled several summers to Trinidad and Tobago to assist in the marking of Integrated Science examination papers for the Caribbean Examination Council. She developed a passion for greater service which fueled by her concern and generosity for others, led her to pursue the Master of Arts Degree in Counselling Psychology at the Caribbean Graduate School of Theology.

She continued her journey to attain a Doctor of Philosophy in Counsellor Education and Supervision from Regent University in Virginia, USA, while managing Strathmore Garden Children's Home. Upon graduating in 2010, she became the first person in Jamaica to have attained such a degree from Regent University.

Having had a wealth of experience and the educational accomplishments, she gained employment on the staff of her Alma Mater—Caribbean Graduate School of Theology where she served as head of the Department of Behavioural Sciences until her passing.

We see clearly from Dr. Stupart's remembrance and achievements that she, too, followed in the footsteps of Dr. Zenas Gerig. She carried the flame of CGST well and equipped others to do the same.

CGST FLAME CARRIER

Mrs. Patricia Eves McKenzie

Graduation: 1996, M.A. in Counselling Psychology
Career: Counselling Psychologist, Educator, Administrator and Motivational Speaker
Birthplace: Jamaica
Married: Rev. Dudley McKenzie
Children: None
Death: March 20, 2021

Mrs. Patricia Eves McKenzie was a renowned-Jamaican Master Christian Educator and counsellor par excellence. In October 2018, the government of Jamaica honoured her by awarding her the Prime Minister's Medal of Appreciation for her service in education. She was the head counsellor at the University of Technology (UTech) in Jamaica until her retirement.

Note: Mrs. Eves McKenzie's profile is compiled from a combination of articles written in the Jamaica Observer and Good News Jamaica, as well as her last interview with Choose Life International on International Women's Day, March 8, 2021.

News of the passing of Mrs. Eves McKenzie saw a flood of tributes on Social Media and elsewhere. She was being hailed as legendary, a mighty woman of God, a virtuous woman of golden character, fashioned by God for a mission to many, an amazing trailblazer, a national icon; the Christian Ms. Lou (referring to Mrs. Louise Bennett Coverley who championed the cause of the Jamaican creole being accepted as an official language. Both women were fluent in English and Jamaican patois and utilized both languages well.)

Many lauded Mrs. Eves McKenzie for her passion for teaching, her wit and commitment to excellence. She was also lauded for Christian service and excellence in the performing arts. As a lecturer at the Jamaica Theological Seminary and during her time with Jamaica Youth for Christ, her use of drama and the performing arts in her work left an indelible mark on the hearts of those with whom she worked and served.

According to Tiffany Janice McLeggon of Good News Jamaica, in an article titled, "Mrs. Patricia Eves McKenzie-A Catalyst for Change," in 1967, the then Ms. Eves graduated from Shortwood Teachers' College after having completed three years. Later that year, she began her career as a Grade Six teacher at the Mona Preparatory School in Kingston.

After a year, she went to work in the public sector during which time she met Reverend Dr. Richmond Nelson, former Principal of the Oberlin High School with whose help she secured a job at Tarrant High School, where she taught English, Spanish and Mathematics.

Before the age of 30, she was a senior teacher at the institution. After nine years of service at Tarrant High, she became the 1st Vice principal of the newly formed high school, Edith Dalton James Secondary High. After a seven-year tenure, in 1984, she took a 10-year hiatus from teaching for other pursuits.

However, her love for teaching never wavered during the time she was away from the classroom. She continued to provide support for children in different subject areas. In her retirement, she beamed with pride concerning her esteemed career in education.

In her own words, in an article in the Jamaica Observer, dated May 18, 2018, Mrs. Eves McKenzie noted:

> I did not leave the profession totally, because I travelled around the island with the team that was adjudicating the inter-schools' debating competitions. I also did a stint with the Children's Own, where I went into schools and helped to train the teachers on how to use the

(publication) in language teaching, so I was not totally away from it.

After strong encouragement from Albert Karram, a leader in her church, she eventually returned to the field of education in January 1994 as principal of Dunrobin High School.

While completing her three-year term as principal, she pursued a master's degree in Counselling Psychology at CGST, and in February 1998, a mere two months after leaving Dunrobin, Mrs. Eves McKenzie commenced lecturing at UTech. She taught subjects in Psychology and continued as a part-time lecturer until October 2001. She also joined the staff of the University's Counselling Centre as a counsellor.

From the article published in the Jamaica Observer, we learnt the following about Mrs. Eves McKenzie's passion for education and helping students. She found the greatest joy in seeing her students do well in their chosen fields, and reaped great satisfaction from seeing them succeed.

Mrs. Eves McKenzie noted: "I have always tried to motivate the students to be their very best in every place that I have been. That has been my mantra, and I feel that I am satisfied that I have seen my students excel."

On the day of the Prime Minister's Medal of Appreciation awards ceremony, she stated,

> I walked into Jamaica House and a gentleman in full khaki police regalia looked at me and said, 'My teacher; you taught me at Tarrant and today you are being

awarded. I am honoured for you'. That made me proud to see him standing there knowing that he is making a meaningful contribution to society.

She further recalled that recently one of her students, whom she had challenged to tap into his true potential, attained his professorship. "He called me and said, 'You have to sit in the front row when I am doing my inaugural lecture.'" She was overwhelmed. "For me, they just need to be their best. That is enough for me."

Mrs. Eves McKenzie told JIS News that she remained in teaching because she felt that she had something to offer. At UTech, she noted, "I would be backstage at graduation when they would get their degrees, sharing their joy, because I know where many of them are coming from. I was always there to say to them, there is another level and they must go for it." And during her retirement, Mrs. Eves

McKenzie continued to help out at UTech, assisting in shaping the lives of her students.

The parallels of Mrs. Eves McKenzie's life and that of Dr. Gerig are unmistakable. This makes her the perfect person to feature in closing this section on outstanding CGST flame carriers.

Similar to Dr. Gerig, Mrs. Eves McKenzie lived a FULL life, and was well-loved. I came to know her personally in 2019, as we shared stages at various women's empowerment conferences. I would speak on enjoying singleness, and she would speak on forgiveness and dealing with unresolved internal wounds and issues that destroy relationships. She championed the cause of celebrating the total woman and living a fulfilled single life.

It is important to note that for many years, Mrs. Eves McKenzie had been the face of singleness in Jamaica. She was a fulfilled single woman who married at the age of 58. Many thought she would never marry and were in total disbelief when she did. In her final interview with Choose Life International on International Women's Day, March 8, 2021, she shed more light on this matter.

During her younger years, she was engaged but the relationship did not work, and over the years she had several suitors but did not find any worthy of her commitment. After recovering from three tiny strokes in 2002, she reasoned with the Lord to show her what He had in mind since he had kept her alive. She also asked God to show her if a man was in the picture and if so, He should show her quickly.

Mrs. Eves McKenzie also reasoned that since her last serious illness was 17 years apart from the recent one, that God needed to give her at least 17 years with a husband. Well God answered her prayers, and she got married on January 1, 2006. She however, did not get 17 years, but 15 beautiful years with her husband Rev. Dudley McKenzie.

During our time of ministering together, she would call me and offer counsel and encouragement when I needed it most. She shared her love story and prayed for me. I believe in a sense she was passing on the baton of Singles ministry to me, and that like her, someday I, too, will marry. I treasure those moments, and our times together will never be forgotten.

In that final, powerful interview with Choose Life International, Mrs. Eves McKenzie noted that she had been a Christian for 56 years (as at February 2021), and spoke about how she made that decision. She came to know the Lord while at Shortwood Teachers' College. The night before she accepted the Lord, there should have been a dance at Jamaica School of Agriculture and she wanted to go. She was a dancer who loved to dance. She requested her leave to attend the dance and the school administration did not give her permission. She was distraught.

At about 5:30 the next morning, a lady made an announcement inviting the ladies to attend an event in the auditorium. In giving the invitation, the lady noted that men would be there, and this excited the young Patricia Eves. At the event, the men of Teen Time sang and David Ho gave the message. When Mr. Ho's preaching was finished, she found herself crying uncontrollably. Then Dr. Hyacinth Peart (nee Webb) asked if she would like to give her heart to the Lord, and she did. That was in February 1965.

Interestingly a year before, she had gone to a party on New Year's Eve and by herself had said to God, "I'd like to be your child this New Year. I don't know how you will make it happen." After accepting the Lord, her friends outrightly told her that if she made that move, they would no longer remain friends. They were serious and true to their word. Notwithstanding, she kept the faith and found new friends. She became part of the Teen Time Camp ministry soon after and later Jamaica Youth For Christ.

I found it interesting that Dr. Peart was there to pray for Mrs. Eves McKenzie in that interview, her final speaking engagement. 12 days later, Mrs. Eves McKenzie passed away on March 20, 2021. It's as if Dr. Peart who had led her in prayer into a new life in Christ 56 years before, was now leading her out of this present life with another prayer.

Like Dr. Gerig, Mrs. Eves McKenzie had several brushes with death. In 1986, she said she was so ill that people thought she would have died, but God kept her. 17 years later as mentioned before, she suffered three tiny strokes and throughout her marriage, she struggled with several illnesses which she did not make public. We are so happy that God kept her alive.

Mrs. Eves McKenzie was also a life-long learner. During her retirement years, before her passing, she was pursuing her doctoral degree. Since her life was an inspiration to many, I'd like to close our tribute to Mrs. Eves McKenzie with the charge she gave in that article in Good News Jamaica in July 2020. They gave us permission to reproduce the article and a transcription of part of the audio from that interview.

The Charge
Set Limits but Don't Limit Yourself

Know yourself. Know your limits. But don't limit yourself. Decide what you want to do and go after it; where you want to reach, go after it. Right now, there's a set of young people who are watching to see if I'm going to finish my doctorate. Because they figure if I can finish it at this age, then they can challenge themselves to do some of the things that they want to do.

Believe in yourself. Okay, everybody doesn't do everything within the same timeframe. I'm thinking some of the young adults might not be married early, and they say Oh, 'it can't happen.' Don't do that to yourself. You never know what the Lord will bring into your life. Let's be prepared. Prepare yourself to live your best life. Yes. Try to understand people and as you understand people, select your friends.

You need people around you who will support you. My friends don't always agree with what I'm about to do, but they will say, I don't agree with that but I support you. You need people who will support you. Be genuine to your friends and they will be genuine.

Remove fear and doubt from your thoughts. Don't be fearful. No, anything that's there, if you set your mind to it, it can be achieved. As I say, it might take a longer time than other people, but that's okay. I remember the dilemma the children I taught at Mona Prep had when I went to university, and they had finished sixth form, and were at university in the same class with me. They weren't sure whether to call me Miss or Patricia. Just understand, your time is your time. Whatever you are doing, put your all into it, and bring other people along with you.

Whatever you learn, pass it on to someone else so his/her life can be better.

Understand that you are a leader in your own right. And as such, you have influence. Wield good influence. Jamaica needs good leaders in every sphere, and see yourself as one who would be a good leader in the sphere that you operate in. Regardless of what the sphere is, just be the best that you can be there. I've said it before and I say it again, do not limit yourself; don't put any limits on your thinking.

No, I'm not saying that you must be stupid, and I'm not saying you must act without clear understanding of end products and all of that. No, I'm not talking about foolish thinking. I'm saying, you have been given a mind and it can be explored. Explore life. Enjoy life. Don't have time and space to grudge or begrudge people. That's a waste of your time. That's a waste of your energy.

Put your time and energy into making the world a better place. All the best.

Part IV

Pass It On

Caribbean Graduate School of Theology

Graduating Class of 2015

CGST's Ambassadors Paying It Forward

"No act of kindness, however small, is ever wasted."
—Aesop

Have you ever examined CGST's logo? An examination of the school's logo will reveal a flame in the center of the logo. I dub it, the flame of transformation and faithful service to church and society for the glory of God. It is the flame of the fire that never says enough, and I want you to catch it and pass it on.

I caught this flame from other CGST flame carriers including my pastor, Rev. Rennard White, and it burned brightly during my time attending both JTS and CGST. Like Dr. Gerig, CGST's flame carriers believe in the development of God's people at the highest standard.

Dr. Gerig and many others have proven that Caribbean people don't need to go overseas to get quality education and good careers. Their efforts have curtailed the brain drain but more needs to be done. Will you join us in this effort?

The flame carriers who redirected me to pursue tertiary education at home did not only encourage me with words, they helped in paying my tuition to attend both schools. Therefore, I believe I have a personal duty to pay it forward.

In fact, in 2019, CGST flame carrier, Dr. Delano Palmer, challenged me to pay it forward when he asked me to consider helping CGST to raise funds. After giving it some thought, I remembered I had offered in 2014 to work with CGST when Dr. Las Newman was the president. I quickly searched my records and found the proposal I had made in that time period. It had been accepted, but unfortunately, I could not follow through because of some personal challenges.

Upon reflection, I realized God was giving me a second chance to pay it forward with Dr. Palmer's request. So, I showed Dr. Corbin, the outgoing president, the initial proposal and offered a new proposal to help. I could lend support using my skill as a writer with a new book series God had placed on my heart titled "Untold Stories."

Dr. Corbin and his team responded enthusiastically. Since he was demitting office as president of CGST, he passed on the baton to Dr. Kerr who diligently followed up. Dr. Kerr, being a CGST graduate, understood the need to pay it forward and is doing so by leading the organization. Both are true CGST ambassadors and flame carriers par excellence.

Now, I want to challenge you to pay it forward if you are a CGST graduate reading this book.

This book chronicles CGST's history and showcases the impact of the institution through the lives of its graduates. It captures the heart of its founder and the flame which burnt brightly in his heart for transformational Christian leadership. Since you have read this far in this book, I am challenging you to become a CGST ambassador and flame carrier. Don't let Dr. Gerig's flame die! Let this vine of God's planting endure to transform more lives.

Recommendations for Paying It Forward

I am using my Authorpreneurial skills. What skills do you have? Perhaps like my pastor and Dr. Black, all you need to do is redirect a young person to CGST for higher Christian education. Like the 2020 graduates, you can share your story and inspire others to consider CGST. Perhaps you can give financially and encourage others to buy this book.

Why not share Dr. Gerig's story and one of the stories of the outstanding graduates? May the Lord lead you creatively!

One of my goals in writing this book is to raise up at least 50 CGST ambassadors who will pass on the flame to others, and join me in raising US$250,000 to help CGST financially.

If 50 ambassadors or readers commit to raise US$5000 in 12-18 months, it's possible!

Another goal is to establish a scholarship fund to help students with the first and final semester outstanding fees. A percentage of the net profits from the book sales will go towards this scholarship.

Funding my tuition was a gift other CGST Flame Carriers gave to me to ensure I finished CGST. Why not follow suit? Let's equip other "called ones" to start and finish their tertiary Christian education, so they can play their part in advancing God's kingdom and the welfare of their country.

Join me in using this book as a tool to recruit new students for CGST and raise financial support for the school.

Having read this book, I urge you to examine your gifts, skills, resources and spheres of influence, and explore how you can use these to partner with CGST to ensure the mission continues.

Will you join the Alumni Association? Will you help the institution become and remain debt free? Can you volunteer your service in administration or become part of the adjunct faculty or staff?

Will you help to pay for a course for a student as Dr. Black did for me?

How about sharing your story of impact and the stories told in this book? Stories never grow old and this is perhaps the easiest way for you to spread Dr. Gerig's flame. It will cost you nothing but time.

If this last option suits you, submit your story to ruthtaylor@extramileja.com to let us know how you have benefitted from CGST or its graduates.

Submit a written testimonial or short 2-minute video to ruthtaylor@extramileja.com. In doing so, tell us when you attended CGST, the programmes pursued, year of graduation, and how CGST has impacted your life and why others should attend.

This will inspire a new generation of students to become part of the CGST story and keep the flame of transformation burning brightly. Will you become a CGST ambassador and flame carrier?

Finally, tell us how this volume of *Untold Stories* has inspired you. Share your feedback by emailing the author at <u>ruthtaylor@extramileja.com</u> or contact her via her website <u>www.extramileja.com</u>.

Share this book with friends, colleagues and family. Help us spread these inspirational stories to the whole world. Let's keep the flame of transformation burning brightly.

Don't forget to leave an honest review on the platform where you bought this book. Thank you.

Untold Stories Trivia

Let's see how much you remember from reading this book.

Answer the questions from Part I and II of the book. If in doubt, review that section of the book to find the answers.

At the end, state your score. Use this trivia as part of your ambassadorial mission as you spread Dr. Gerig's flame.

Part I

It Only Takes a Spark

1. At what age did Dr. Gerig give his life to God? _____/1

2. What were the two miraculous events that took place early in Dr. Gerig's life?   _____/2

3. When did Dr. Gerig move to Jamaica?   _____/1

4. In what year did Dr. Gerig receive the Order of Distinction from the government of Jamaica? _____/1

5. How many years did Dr. Gerig serve as president of CGST? _____/1

6. How many countries did he visit in his work to get the institutions accredited? _____/1

7. When did Dr. Gerig die?_____/1

8. Which of his sons currently serves on the CGST Board in 2021?   _____/1

9. How long did he serve in Jamaica with the Missionary Church Association? _____/1

Total   _____/10

PART II

CGST: A Guardian of the Flame

1. Name all the Caribbean presidents of CGST 1992-2021 and the time period each served? _____/8

2. In what year did CGST start? _____/1

3. How many students enrolled at the beginning? _____/1

4. Name the degree programmes offered in the first two years?   _____/1

5. How many students graduated from the first batch? _____/1

6. Name two of first graduates and the programme each did?   _____/4

7. How many honorary doctoral degrees has CGST conferred up to 2020? _____/1

8. Name three of the degree programmes no longer done at CGST in 2021? _____/3

Total _____/20

Overall Score _____/30

Grateful Acknowledgements

I am grateful to God for His clear guidance to publish this book.

To Dr. David Corbin, who enthusiastically supported this project, and skillfully guided our discussions with wisdom and grace, thank you for commencing the work and passing on the baton to Dr. Kerr. Your endorsement has been invaluable.

To Dr. Viviene Kerr, thank you for so masterfully connecting the dots, allaying my fears and giving me the accountability and support I needed to bring this God-given vision to pass. Without your gentle nudges and persistence, this project may have been aborted.

To the CGST staff who worked diligently on the project—Candice Reynolds and Jodi-Ann Gilpin, thank you for your invaluable contribution to the process in contacting the graduates, offering encouraging words and accountability. Your gentle nudges motivated me to finish.

To Dr. Sheldon Campbell, thanks for being part of the initial discussions to make this project a reality.

To Stan Gerig, thank you for the role you and your family played in the life of CGST and in this project. Thank you for the vital articles, data correction and your gracious foreword.

To Mrs. Cecilia Spencer, thank you for the archival role you have played in preserving the record of activities of CGST through the library, and providing just what we needed to get the story correct.

To the four 2020 graduates who shared their testimonies of impact, and the outstanding graduate flame carriers, thank you for letting your light shine and demonstrating that Dr. Gerig's flame still burns brightly. You have followed well in the footsteps of Dr. Zenas Gerig.

To Dr. Palmer, whose writings captured Dr. Gerig's untold story, thank you for showing the importance of writing and preserving this magnificent story. Your journal entry made this book possible. Thank you for also asking me to help CGST.

To my pastor, Rev. Rennard White, and Dr. Dameon Black, thank you for your critical role in being God's hand of redirection, and pointing me to the schools established by Dr. Gerig. Without your input, this book would not have been possible.

To Ms. Grace Gordon, I am so grateful that God assigned you to this project to ensure a beautiful finish with your editorial skills. Thank you for fact checking and bringing greater clarity of thought to the written material.

To my cover designer, Adedolapo, thank you for your part in making this a beautiful product.

To CGST's ambassadors, and all who will purchase this book to carry the flame of transformation, thank you. May this vine of God's planting forever endure!

About the Author

Cameka "Ruth" Taylor is a proud graduate of CGST and a Jamaican Authorpreneur. She has over 20 years of experience in teaching from the Early Childhood to the Tertiary Level of the education system in Jamaica.

Ruth is an Amazon bestselling author of over 20 books. She makes a full-time living from her writing and the income streams it generates.

Ruth is on a mission to ensure fewer books die in the minds of their authors, that more manuscripts become published legacies and precious lives are transformed with the turn of each page.

Her vision is to raise up 10,000 Caribbean Authorpreneurs by 2030 who will declare God's glory among the nations, and leverage books to advance the cause of the kingdom, non-profit institutions and bring personal, spiritual and financial transformation to their lives and the lives of others.

Through her Authorpreneurship Academy and podcast, Ruth teaches and coaches published and aspiring authors how to multiply their impact and income with non-fiction books.

With over 17 years of speaking and travelling experience across 14 countries thus far, Ruth continues to activate, educate and empower thousands of people in Jamaica, other countries in the Caribbean region, Latin America and Africa to win in their personal, professional and spiritual lives for the glory of God.

Contact her at ruthtaylor@extramileja.com if you need her coaching services.

NOTE: If you found this material helpful, please submit a review on the platform where you purchased it. You can also send feedback to the author. Thank you.

To support CGST, contact the school via their website at https://cgst.edu.jm/.

Resources by
C. Ruth Taylor

Visit www.extramileja.com to get a free e-copy of "The Rocket-Writer" which will help you to write your non-fiction book faster than you think.

For Indie publishing support, join our free Facebook tribe "Indie Authorpreneurs" to learn how to publish on a budget, create multiple income streams and impact more lives with books. Upon joining, you will get a 1-page pre-publishing checklist and other goodies.

Visit www.authorpreneursecrets.com to check out our podcast and kick start your Authorpreneurship journey.

Other Publications
by C. Ruth Taylor

1. *Authorpreneur Secret$*: Write Fast. Publish Affordably and Generate Lasting Income

2. *Pen It to Win It*: Going Beyond Book Sales

3. *Design to Win Road Map*: Your Winning Life and Career Compass

4. *Unshackled Queen*: From Heartbreak to Wholeness

5. *Shaped for Purpose:* Reflections on Life Experiences and Purpose.

You can find these and Ruth's other books at www.extramileja.com/ruthsbookshop.

References

Choose Life International. (2021 March 8). CLI Webinar #98 – Keys to Increased Happiness – International Women's Day featured Mrs. Patricia Eves McKenzie. https://www.youtube.com/watch?v=HM0WOBk0wuU

Grand Rapids Press. (2011). Dr. Zenas Gerig Obituary. Grand Rapids, Michigan. https://www.legacy.com/obituaries/name/zenas-gerig-obituary?pid=153727080

Ham, Shirley. (2001, December 6). Couple return after lifetime Jamaican mission. *KPM News. Kendaville, Indiana.* https://www.kpcnews.com/article 9-7c58-50b6-968f-e21bdadedae2.html

Jamaica Gleaner Newspaper Archives. Zenas Gerig. 46 records for Zenas Gerig, Publication Title: Kingston Gleaner. Dr. Gerig's name is mentioned from 1959-2011. *Kingston Gleaner.* https://gleaner.newspaperarchive.com/tags/zenas-gerig/

Jamaica Gleaner Newspaper Archives (2001 April 15, 2001). A zeal for God: A church for poor people.

Jamaica Gleaner Newspaper.
https://gleaner.newspaperarchive.com/kingston-gleaner/2001-04-15/page-80/

Jamaican Gleaner Archives. (2011, Sunday, October 23) Kingston. *Kingston Gleaner (Newspaper)* Caribbean Graduate School of Theology 25th Anniversary (featured article).

Jamaica Gleaner Newspaper Archives (1996 May 13). Article on Jamaica Theological Seminary.

Jamaica Gleaner Archives. (1967, Wednesday, June 14). Article on Jamaica Theological Seminary. *Kingston Gleaner (Newspaper).*

Jamaica Observer. (2020 June 30). Caribbean Graduate School of Theology gets first female president. https://www.jamaicaobserver.com/news/caribbean-graduate-school-of-theology-gets-first-female-president_197209

Jamaica Information Service. (2018 May 21) Celebrating Patricia Eves-McKenzie, Retired Counselor, Medical Centre, UTech, Jamaica. *Jamaica Observer.* https://www.jamaicaobserver.com/news/teaching-is-my-first-love-says-pm-award-recipient_133488?profile=1373

McLeggon. Tiffany J. (2020 July 1). Patricia Eves-McKenzie – Catalyst for Change. *Good New Jamaica.*

https://goodnewsjamaica.com/index.php/2020/07/
01/patricia-eves-mckenzie-catalystforchange/?
=IwAR2K7IquDoWizlKIFcfppypknZ-
M4TWKFcC4B9VOxlbiX57T8dHIZH2F_FO

Palmer, Vincent D. 2002. Caribbean Journal of Evangelical
Theology (CJET). Tribute to the Gerigs: A Sequel. 73-80

Ringenberg, Roger. 1992. A History of Jamaica Theological
Seminary: 1960-1992. PhD. diss., Trinity International
University

Made in the USA
Columbia, SC
29 June 2021